100 Glues, Brews, and Goos

100 Glues, Brews, and Goos

Kid-Tested Activities That Stimulate Creativity and Critical Thinking

Diana F. Marks

Illustrated by Donna L. Farrell

BLOOMSBURY LIBRARIES UNLIMITED
NEW YORK · LONDON · OXFORD · NEW DELHI · SYDNEY

BLOOMSBURY LIBRARIES UNLIMITED
Bloomsbury Publishing Inc
1385 Broadway, New York, NY 10018, USA
50 Bedford Square, London, WC1B 3DP, UK
29 Earlsfort Terrace, Dublin 2, Ireland

BLOOMSBURY, BLOOMSBURY LIBRARIES UNLIMITED and the Diana logo are
trademarks of Bloomsbury Publishing Plc

First published in the United States of America 2025

Copyright © Diana F. Marks, 2025

Cover images: Child with scissors © Seventyfour/Adobe Stock; Purple Goo © GreenSkyStudio/Adobe Stock;
Child sewing © M-image/Adobe Stock; Arts and Craft Materials © yulia Petrova /Alamy

All rights reserved. No part of this publication may be reproduced or transmitted in any form or
by any means, electronic or mechanical, including photocopying, recording, or any information storage
or retrieval system, without prior permission in writing from the publishers.

Bloomsbury Publishing Inc does not have any control over, or responsibility for, any third-party
websites referred to or in this book. All internet addresses given in this book were correct at the time
of going to press. The author and publisher regret any inconvenience caused if addresses have
changed or sites have ceased to exist, but can accept no responsibility for any such changes.

The publisher has done its best to make sure the instructions and/or recipes in this book are correct.
However, users should apply judgment and experience when preparing recipes, especially parents
and teachers working with young people. The publisher accepts no responsibility for the outcome
of any recipe included in this volume and assumes no liability for, and is released by readers from, any
injury or damage resulting from the strict adherence to, or deviation from, the directions and/or recipes
herein. The publisher is not responsible for any reader's specific health or allergy needs that
may require medical supervision, nor for any adverse reactions to the recipes contained
in this book. All yields are approximations.

Library of Congress Cataloging-in-Publication Data
Names: Marks, Diana F., author.
Title: 100 glues, brews, and goos : kid-tested activities that stimulate creativity
and critical thinking / Diana F. Marks ; Illustrated by Donna L. Farrell.
Description: New York, NY : Bloomsbury Libraries Unlimited, 2025. | Includes bibliographical references.
Identifiers: LCCN 2024032401 (print) | LCCN 2024032402 (ebook) | ISBN 9798216190127 (paperback) |
ISBN 9798216190134 (epub) | ISBN 9798216190141 (pdf)
Subjects: LCSH: Activity programs in education. | Creative activities and seat work. |
Student-centered learning. | Critical thinking in children.
Classification: LCC LB1027.25 .M258 2025 (print) | LCC LB1027.25 (ebook) | DDC 371.3–dc23/eng/20240814
LC record available at https://lccn.loc.gov/2024032401
LC ebook record available at https://lccn.loc.gov/2024032402

ISBN: PB: 979-8-2161-9012-7
       ePDF: 979-8-2161-9014-1
       eBook: 979-8-2161-9013-4

Typeset by Integra Software Services Pvt. Ltd.

To find out more about our authors and books visit www.bloomsbury.com
and sign up for our newsletters.

Contents

Acknowledgments — ix
Introduction — x
Tips — xii

1 LET'S BE BUBBLEOLOGISTS! — 1
Best Bubble Solution — 2
Bubble Frame 1 (Pipe Cleaners) — 3
Bubble Frame 2 (Straws and Strings) — 4
Tabletop Bubbles — 5
Liquid-Filled Bubbles — 6

2 LET'S BE CRYSTALLOGRAPHERS! — 7
Basic Crystal Procedure with Chart for 8 Types of Crystals — 8
Epsom Salt Frost — 10
Borax Stalagmites and Stalactites — 11
Crystal Garden — 12
Homemade Geodes — 13

3 LET'S BE CRYPTOLOGISTS! — 14
Invisible Ink 1 (Juice Invisible Ink) — 15
Invisible Ink 2 (Vegetable Oil and Ammonia Invisible Ink) — 16
Invisible Ink 3 (Table Salt Invisible Ink) — 17
Invisible Ink 4 (Wax Invisible Ink) — 18
Invisible Ink 5 (Baking Soda Invisible Ink) — 19

4 LET'S BE SLIMEOLOGISTS! — 20
Non-Newtonian Fluid 1 (Cornstarch and Water) — 21
Non-Newtonian Fluid 2 (White Glue and Liquid Starch) — 22
Non-Newtonian Fluid 3 (White Glue and Contact Lens Solution) — 23
Non-Newtonian Fluid 4 (White Glue and Borax) — 24
Non-Newtonian Fluid 5 (Sculpting Material) — 25

5 LET'S BE GOO-OLOGISTS! — 27
- Stretchers — 28
- Fake Plastic — 29
- Epsom Salt Goo — 30
- Squeeze Goo — 31
- Gelatin Strings — 32

6 LET'S BE BIOSCRAPOLOGISTS! — 33
- Carrot Plant (Root Vegetable Plant) — 34
- Romaine Lettuce Plant (Base Plant) — 35
- Plants from Seeds — 36
- Sweet Potato Plant — 37
- Potato Plant — 38

7 LET'S BE ORNITHOLOGISTS! — 39
- Homemade Bird Seed Mixture — 42
- Bird Food 1 (Food Balls for Birds) — 43
- Bird Food 2 (Kabobs for Birds) — 44
- Birds' Holiday Tree — 45
- Hummingbird Brew — 46

8 LET'S BE ENTOMOLOGISTS! — 47
- Food for All Kinds of Bugs — 48
- Moth Attractor Goo — 49
- Butterfly Brew — 50
- Ladybug Hotel — 51
- Worm Farm — 52

9 LET'S BE VULCANOLOGISTS! — 54
- Volcano Model — 55
- Volcanic Action 1 (Strombolian Eruption) — 56
- Volcanic Action 2 (Hawaiian Eruption) — 57
- Volcanic Action 3 (Vulcanian Eruption) — 58
- Volcanic Action 4 (Peléan Eruption) — 59

10 LET'S BE PALEONTOLOGISTS! — 60
- Mold and Cast Fossil — 61
- Trace Fossil (Dinosaur Footprints) — 63

	Carbon Film Fossil	64
	Fossil Eggs	65
	Amber with Inclusions	66

11 LET'S BE HYDROLOGISTS! — 68
    Amazing Water 1 (Demonstration of Adhesion and Cohesion) — 69
    Amazing Water 2 (Another Demonstration of Adhesion and Cohesion) — 70
    Ocean in a Bottle — 71
    Homemade Cloud — 72
    Layers of Liquid — 73

12 LET'S BE MUSICOLOGISTS! — 74
    Water Glass Musical Instruments — 75
    Kazoo — 76
    Tambourines — 77
    Rubber Band Guitar — 78
    Steel Drums — 79

13 LET'S BE TIME TRAVELERS! — 80
    Yarn Dolls — 81
    Cup and Ball Toy — 82
    Humming Whirligig Toy — 83
    Quill Pen — 84
    Berry Ink — 85

14 LET'S BE ARTISTS! — 86
    Fresco — 87
    Mosaic — 88
    Simple Loom — 89
    Potato Stamps — 91
    Vegetable and Fruit Stamps — 92

15 LET'S BE CHROMATOLOGISTS! — 93
    Classic Finger Paint — 94
    Versatile Paint — 95
    Milk Paint — 96
    Egg Tempera Paint — 97
    Pan Paints — 98

16 LET'S BE CLAYOLOGISTS! — 99
- Silly Stuff — 100
- Playful Plastic — 101
- Flour Clay — 102
- Frozen Bread Molding Material — 103
- Cinnamon Dough — 104

17 LET'S BE PAPER CHEMISTS! — 106
- Traditional Rectangular Mold and Deckle — 107
- Basic Recycled Paper — 108
- Decorative Paper Containers — 109
- Deckled Paper — 110
- Aged Paper — 111

18 LET'S BE PAPER ENGINEERS! — 112
- Pinwheel — 113
- Vertical Spinners — 114
- Horizontal Spinners — 115
- Paper Wreath or Star or Flower — 116
- Origami Fortune Teller — 117

19 LET'S BE CRAFTERS! — 119
- Scratch-and-Sniff Paints — 120
- Scratch-Off Projects — 121
- Colored Glues and/or Glitter Glues — 122
- Make Your Own Stickers — 123
- Snow Globe — 124

20 LET'S BE WACKADOODLE SCIENTISTS! — 125
- Candy-Diet Soda Eruption — 126
- Dancing Raisins — 127
- Balloon Rocket — 128
- Straw Rocket — 129
- Simple Telephones — 130

Bibliography — 131

Acknowledgments

I thank my husband, Peter, for his patience and understanding.

I thank our sons, Kevin and Colin, for their support and encouragement.

I thank our three delightful grandchildren, Evelyn, Adelynn, and Ethan, for their hugs and kisses.

I thank Donna L. Farrell for her artistic expertise and her wonderful illustrations.

Introduction

Welcome to *100 Glues, Brews, and Goos: Kid-Tested Activities That Stimulate Creativity and Critical Thinking*! This book has been waiting for you!

I am very fortunate. A few years ago, my book *The BIG Book of Glues, Brews, and Goos: 500+ Kid-Tested Recipes and Formulas for Hands-On Learning* was published. It was a compilation of two previous books. Now I have written a new book, a selection of 100 wonderful activities to encourage critical thinking and creativity.

This book is designed differently from the previous book. The previous book was more like an encyclopedia, providing many, many formulas that you could choose from. This book provides 20 interesting and exciting topics, and each topic provides 5 activities with many, many suggested adaptations. I have also provided a culminating activity for each chapter.

This book is designed to encourage critical thinking and creativity. The main theme of this book is *What if* … For example, *What if* we use a different type of dish soap for our bubble solution? *What if* we add more paper clips to our vertical spinner? *What if* we write an invisible ink message with a 1776-style quill pen? That theme of *What if* … encourages children to think deeply and originally. So encourage all those *What if* suggestions. And prepare for those *What ifs.* However, before the *What if* is executed, ask your young loved one to predict the results. What will happen and why? The best that can happen is that your child will be right. Successful predictions bring joy. The worst that could happen is that your loved one's prediction is wrong. Learning to deal with wrong is a good life skill. Keep a journal, note those predictions, and record the results.

This book is designed to stimulate the imaginations of children from a variety of age levels. Try the activities with young ones and then try them again when those young ones are older. Those *What if* suggestions get better over time.

This book is designed to provide solutions to problems your child might face. Does your child need an Earth Day project? No problem, several chapters can provide help. Need a science fair project? Your child is covered. Need a Father's Day gift? Several different options are available. Of course, these activities are great just for a rainy day or for a child recovering from an ear infection or for a way just to fight boredom.

This book is designed with your ease in mind. Materials are easily accessible and easy to use. I have also tried to make clean up easy. Finally, I have included further activities that should occupy your young loved one without burdening you. I suggest you keep a stash of some of the most-used materials, including white glue, white vinegar, and baking soda. You don't want to run out of baking soda when you are trying to replicate a Strombolian volcanic eruption!

This book is designed to demonstrate that art is composed of a great deal of science and that science is composed of a great deal of art. For example, we see the color red from a red paint because the paint absorbs all the spectrum colors except red and thus reflects the color red. Going in the other direction, that science is composed of a great deal of art, the musicology chapter demonstrates that we can learn about sound by creating music.

This book is designed to be well-used, dog-eared, and marked-up. I hope you and yours enjoy this book. I hope your young one becomes the better for participating in these activities, and becomes an inquisitive, accomplished, and caring learner.

Tips

Make safety the top priority. Try to anticipate any possible problems and eliminate all dangers. Review safety procedures with students.

Only 1 of these 100 activities is meant to be eaten; ensure that children consume only what you want them to eat or drink. Even materials such as flour or sugar in these activities should not be ingested.

Know where the nearest fire extinguisher is and how to use it. Keep a first aid kit nearby.

Always test a formula before using it with children.

Carefully read through the entire activity before beginning.

Make sure all materials are assembled before beginning a project.

Keep pots, spoons, and utensils used for making food separate from those used in nonfood projects.

Keep plenty of hot pads, old towels, paper towels, and wipes around. You can never anticipate everything when children and good times get together.

Children should wear protective clothing. Smocks, old shirts, and aprons add to the fun. Lab coats would be such an inspiration! Keep some safety goggles and rubber gloves around just to be super careful.

Discard all unused materials in the trash. Some formulas, such as the slimes group, could clog plumbing. Make sure any heated materials have cooled before discarding them.

Activities note when a stove or heating element is required. However, microwave ovens, toaster ovens, electric frying pans, and slow cookers could be more useful and easier to clean up.

Sometimes hot running water is not available. Cleaning up, therefore, can be difficult. If running water is not available, use plastic bags to hold ingredients instead of mixing bowls. Students like to seal the bags and mix the contents by squeezing. Although plastic bags are not the most environmentally preferred material, their use may make the difference between carrying out a project or dismissing it as too cumbersome.

Always keep a few pens, with different color inks, around to write in this book. Keep notes on what works and what does not work with your children. Even better, encourage your children to add their notes or comments. Remember that a well-used, liquid-stained, dog-eared book is a treasure!

Treasure these times as well. Marvel, create, and often ask *What if ...!*

1 Let's Be Bubbleologists!

Something as simple as blowing bubbles can create great fun and wonderful science. Children could create all kinds of bubble solutions and all kinds of bubble frames and record the results. Good bubble solutions follow several rules. Most bubble solutions should be made days ahead, preferably even a week ahead, of use. Bubble solutions should be at room temperature. Use distilled water whenever possible. The size of the bubbles depends on such factors as humidity and air circulation. Also, the science seems to be that less is more where bubbles are concerned. In other words, the less dishwashing liquid used, the bigger the bubbles. The first 3 activities should be done outside.

BEST BUBBLE SOLUTION

[Makes 1 cup]

Pre-Activity: Glycerin, available at most pharmacies, extends the life of bubbles. Other viscous liquids, such as light corn syrup, honey, and vegetable oil, also work.

Materials

- ✓ ⅔ cup water, preferably distilled
- ✓ ⅓ cup dishwashing liquid
- ✓ 1 teaspoon glycerin
- ✓ mixing bowl
- ✓ mixing spoon
- ✓ airtight storage container

Procedure

1. Mix water, dishwashing liquid, and glycerin together.
2. Pour into airtight storage container. Allow it to age at room temperature for a few days if possible.
3. Blow those bubbles!

Post-Activity: **What if** other brands of dishwashing liquid are used? **What if** other types of soaps (for example, shampoo, liquid hand soap) are used? **What if** other viscous liquids (for example, light corn syrup, honey) are substituted for the glycerin? **What if** bubbles are blown under different weather conditions (for example, cold days, breezy days, hot days, dry days)?

BUBBLE FRAME 1 (PIPE CLEANERS)

Pre-Activity: Plastic bubble wands found in commercial bubble solutions are just a beginning to this creative process. Bubble frames can be 3-dimensional or square-edged or both. No matter the shape of the frame, the bubbles will always be spherical. Pipe cleaners easily bend, and bright colors add to the fun. Beads could be added to give the bubble frames even more jazz.

Materials

✓ pipe cleaners, 18 inches long
✓ bucket of bubble solution

Procedure

1. Make simple frames such as those found in commercial bubble bottles. Try out the frames.
2. Make frames of various shapes (square, triangular, 3-dimensional, etc.).
3. Place frames in bucket of bubble solution. Allow solution to really cover frames. Remove frames from solution and see what happens! Record what works and what does not work.

Post-Activity: Make a very large frame from multiple pipe cleaners. Have a contest to see who can make the biggest bubble.

Another Post-Activity: What else could become bubble wands? Funnels? Bundles of straws? Plastic cups with holes in the bottom? What else? Make a list of what works and what does not.

BUBBLE FRAME 2 (STRAWS AND STRINGS)

Pre-Activity: Science becomes fun with this rectangular but flexible bubble frame. Not only can children blow bubbles, but they can also manipulate the shape of the frame and thus the bubble film.

Materials

- 2 straws per child
- 1 40-inch length of string per child
- shallow rectangular pans filled with bubble solution

Procedure

1. Thread the string through one straw and then through the other.
2. Tie the ends of the string together so that a continuous loop of string has been formed.
3. Force the knot into one of the straws and pull the straws away from each other.
4. The resulting bubble frame is a rectangular shape with straws on the sides and strings on top and bottom.
5. Place bubble frames in rectangular pan of bubble solution. Allow solution to really soak into strings and straws.
6. Remove frames from solution and play. A bubble film will form inside the frame. Twist, contort, and compress each frame. The bubble solution does amazing things.
7. If children get their hands very wet from the bubble solution, they can pass their hands through the frame's bubble film.

Post-Activity: Make a large bubble frame using plastic tubing and heavy-duty string. How big a bubble did the frame make?

TABLETOP BUBBLES

Pre-Activity: Children's work areas have never been as clean as they will be after this experiment! Remember that bubbles break when they encounter "dry." The tables can get messy.

Materials

- ✓ nonporous tabletops
- ✓ bubble solution
- ✓ wide straws
- ✓ spoon

Procedure

1. Give each child a straw.
2. Pour about a tablespoon of bubble solution on table in front of each child. Smear the bubble solution around so that it occupies an area of a large dinner plate.
3. Instruct child to put one end of straw into bubble solution and blow through the other end. Make sure bubble end of straw is really saturated with bubble solution.
4. With practice, children can make bubbles bigger than dinner plates. They can also make bubbles inside bubbles and bubble chains.
5. If a child is having difficulty getting a bubble started, swirl the solution around until a small bubble forms. Then the child can pierce the small bubble with the straw and blow slowly.

Post-Activity: Children can measure the diameter of their bubbles after the bubbles break by looking at the ring left behind. This could lead into some research on biggest bubbles ever made, or why bubbles are always spherical, or would bubbles form in a vacuum.

LIQUID-FILLED BUBBLES

[Makes 1 batch]

Pre-Activity: The liquid-filled bubbles actually have a layer of air surrounding them. This layer keeps the liquid inside from spreading into the surrounding liquid.

Materials

- ½ cup light corn syrup
- 1 cup water
- 2 teaspoons dishwashing liquid
- 4 drops food coloring
- ½ teaspoon salt
- 1 glass bowl
- 1 measuring cup
- 1 clean, empty squeeze bottle

Procedure

1. Pour light corn syrup into the bottom of the glass bowl. This layer will hopefully protect the liquid-filled bubbles as they fall.
2. Gently pour water into the bowl.
3. Add dishwashing liquid and gently swirl mixture to distribute.
4. Use measuring cup to scoop out some of the water-dishwashing liquid mixture.
5. Add food coloring to water in the measuring cup. The color will help you see the liquid-filled bubbles. Add the salt.
6. Pour salt-food coloring-water-dishwashing liquid into squeeze bottle and screw on the top.
7. Hold the opening of the squeeze bottle vertical to the bowl and gently squeeze.
8. Some of the liquid-filled bubbles will fall below the surface of the water in the bowl.
9. Children have fun watching the bubbles sink and then rise to the surface.

Post-Activity: Children could try the same activity by omitting either the light corn syrup or salt. What happens? Could another viscous fluid, such as honey or vegetable oil, be substituted for the light corn syrup?

Bubbleology Culminating Activity

Children could take some photos of their experiments and make a slide-show presentation.

2 Let's Be Crystallographers!

Crystals are easy to produce, and children like to see the changes. The two main ingredients for crystal growing are the chemical (solute) and water (solvent). A saturated solution is made by dissolving as much of the chemical, or crystal material, as possible in boiling water. When the solution cools, it becomes supersaturated. Crystals are by-products of this supersaturation. Crystal solutions should not be disturbed (stirred, shaken, moved) after they are made.

BASIC CRYSTAL PROCEDURE WITH CHART FOR 8 TYPES OF CRYSTALS

Pre-Activity: Many crystals contain substances that should not be eaten. Also, many crystals are slow to grow; days can pass before changes can be observed.

Crystal	Chemical Name	Chemical Formula	Ratio of Substance to Water	Notes
Salt	Sodium chloride	$NaCl$	1 ½ cups salt to 1 cup water	Easiest to grow
Sugar	Sucrose	$C_{12}H_{22}O_{11}$	3 cups sugar to 1 cup water	Not always successful
Epsom salt	Magnesium sulfate	$MgSO_4$	⅔ cup Epsom salt to 1 cup water	Epsom salt bath bombs would be great presents
Baking soda	Sodium bicarbonate	$NaHCO_3$	⅓ cup baking soda to 1 cup water	Baking soda is found in baking section of grocery store
Washing soda	Sodium carbonate	Na_2CO_3	⅔ cup washing soda to 1 cup water	Washing soda can be found in laundry section of grocery store
Borax	Sodium tetraborate	$Na_2B_4O_7$	⅔ cup borax to 1 cup water	Borax should not be consumed
Cream of tartar	Potassium bitartrate	$KHC_4H_4O_6$	⅔ cup cream of tartar to 1 cup water	Cream of tartar can be found in spice section of grocery store
Alum	Aluminum potassium sulfate	$AlK(SO_4)_2$	2 ounces alum to 1 cup water	Alum can be found in spice section of grocery store

Materials

- ✓ amount of solute from above chart
- ✓ amount of water from above chart
- ✓ stove or heating element
- ✓ pot and hot pads
- ✓ mixing spoon
- ✓ heat-resistant jar (e.g., canning jar)
- ✓ string
- ✓ paper clip, nail, or other small weight
- ✓ pencil or stick longer than the diameter of the jar

Procedure

1. Heat water to boiling.
2. Gradually add some solute and stir. Keep solution boiling.
3. Add more solute and stir. Repeat until solute will no longer dissolve.
4. Remove pot from stove. Using hot pads, pour solution carefully into jar.
5. Cut a piece of string longer than the height of the jar. Tie one end to a pencil or stick. Tie the other end to paper clip or small weight.
6. Place pencil across top of jar so that string and weight dangle into salt solution.
7. Put the jar in a place where it will not be disturbed. Soon crystals will grow on string.

Post-Activity: **What if** instead of using a boring bit of string, a crystal star or a crystal critter was used? An 18-inch pipe cleaner could be bent in just about any shape. Just leave enough pipe cleaner to loop over the pencil.

Another Post-Activity: Consider combining two different solutes, for example salt and sugar. What are the results?

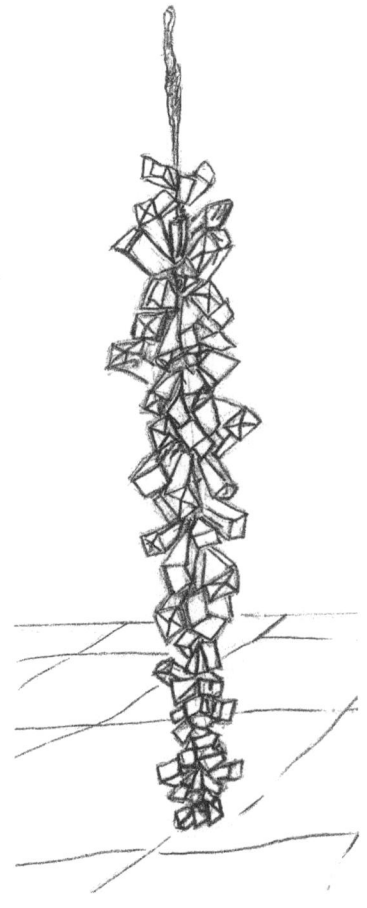

EPSOM SALT FROST

[Makes 2 cups]

Pre-Activity: The liquid dishwashing detergent binds the Epsom salt to the glass. It also allows easy cleaning. Could children paint a simple picture, like a snowflake or a snowman?

Materials

- 1 cup Epsom salt
- 1 ½ cups water
- stove or heating element
- 3 tablespoons liquid dishwashing detergent
- pot and hot pads
- mixing spoon
- paintbrush
- window or other glass surface

Procedure

1. Heat water to boiling.
2. Gradually add some Epsom salt and stir. Keep solution boiling.
3. Add more Epsom salt and stir. Repeat until Epsom salt will no longer dissolve.
4. Remove pot from stove.
5. Add liquid dishwashing detergent.
6. Let mixture cool.
7. Paint solution on window or glass with paintbrush. When solution dries, needle-like fan patterns will appear.
8. To clean, use soap and water to remove the Epsom salt frost.

Post-Activity: **What if** the solution is divided into several small containers and different food coloring is added to each container? Does the resulting painting look like stained glass?

BORAX STALAGMITES AND STALACTITES

[Makes 3 cups]

Pre-Activity: Natural stalagmites and stalactites form in caves when water, carrying dissolved calcium carbonate, finds its way into the interior. The water evaporates, but the calcium carbonate stays, sometimes creating these formations. An easy way to remember which is which is that stalaGtites has a *G* for *Ground*. StalaCtites has a *C* for *Ceiling*. These kid-created formations are not always a guarantee. Sometimes the string dries out, ending the process.

Materials

- 1 ⅓ cups borax*
- 1 ½ cups water
- stove or heating element
- pot and hot pads
- mixing spoon
- 2 small, heat-resistant jars (e.g., canning jars) of the same size
- several 12-inch pieces of lightweight string
- tray, big enough to hold both jars, with 3 inches of space between them

Borax, as with almost all materials in this book, should not be eaten. Watch small children closely when they make this formula.

Procedure

1. Heat water to boiling.
2. Gradually add some borax and stir. Keep solution boiling.
3. Add more borax and stir. Repeat until borax will no longer dissolve.
4. Remove pot from stove. Using hot pads, take pot off stove.
5. Place the jars on a tray 3 inches apart.
6. Divide solution between the jars.
7. Soak strings for 2 minutes in one of the jars.
8. Place one end of each string in the solution of one jar.
9. Place the other end of each string in the solution of the other jar. The strings are thus suspended between jars.
10. Solution will begin to flow along strings. Some of the solution will drip from strings and solidify. Stalagmites and stalactites will form. Sometimes the two features will join and form a column of borax crystal material.

Post-Activity: **What if** different crystal solutions, or blends of different crystal solutions, are used? **What if** food coloring is added? **What if** jar solutions are different from each other?

CRYSTAL GARDEN

[Makes 1 crystal garden]

> **Pre-Activity**: Children have been making crystal gardens for many generations. Now one of the ingredients, laundry bluing, is hard to find. Sometimes you can find it in a grocery store, or you can order it on the Internet. The recipe will work without the bluing, but the results will not be as dramatic. Pieces of sponge work just as well as charcoal and are much cleaner.

Materials

- several walnut-size pieces of charcoal or sponge
- 1 quart water
- petroleum jelly
- glass pie pan
- 6 tablespoons salt with no added iodine
- 6 tablespoons water
- 6 tablespoons liquid laundry bluing*
- 2 tablespoons ammonia*
- food coloring
- mixing bowl
- mixing spoon

The use of laundry bluing and ammonia must be monitored closely. Neither liquid should be ingested.

Procedure

1. Soak pieces of charcoal or sponge in 1 quart water for 20 minutes.
2. Coat edge of glass pie pan with petroleum jelly to keep crystals in dish.
3. Place pieces of charcoal or sponge in glass pie pan.
4. Mix all the other ingredients except food coloring in mixing bowl. Make sure salt is dissolved.
5. Pour solution over pieces of charcoal or sponge.
6. Dot surface with food coloring.
7. Do not move glass pie plate. Delicate crystals should start to appear in 20 minutes.

> **Post-Activity**: **What if** a plastic pan is substituted for the glass pie plate? **What if** petroleum jelly is left out of the procedure? **What if** Epsom salt is substituted for salt?

HOMEMADE GEODES

[Makes 12]

> **Pre-Activity**: Natural geodes begin during volcanic eruptions. Lava cools around air bubbles, forming hollow rocks. Water, bringing minerals, seeps into the hollow rocks. Over time the water leaves, but the minerals remain and begin to form crystals. The larger the crystals are, the older the geode is. Children enjoy making these shiny gems. If kept dry, the crystals can last quite a long time.

Materials

- 1 empty, clean egg carton
- plastic wrap
- scissors
- clean, empty egg shells
- supersaturated solution of salt or Epsom salt (see page 8)

Procedure

1. Cut plastic wrap into 12 pieces and line each of the 12 depressions in the egg carton.
2. Place an egg shell in each depression.
3. Pour some supersaturated solution into each of the egg shells.
4. Let mixture sit for several days. The egg shells should start to look like geodes.

> **Post-Activity**: The most valued geode crystals are black. What combination of food colorings will make the geodes black?

Crystallography Culminating Activity

Children could rank their favorite crystals and explain how they decided on the rankings.

3 Let's Be Cryptologists!

Cryptologists figure out ways to send hidden messages, and one of those ways is to use invisible inks. Invisible inks have been around for thousands of years; the ancient Greeks and Romans used them. Some invisible inks are chemical reactions. For example, a base reacts to an acid. Other invisible inks use heat to bring out an invisible message. In this chapter I have coupled invisible inks with other projects to make treasure maps or spy codes.

INVISIBLE INK 1 (JUICE INVISIBLE INK)

[Makes ½ cup]

Pre-Activity: Children enjoy experimenting with different solutions. The liquid materials are quite safe. Children should be supervised when they use the light bulb. A warm iron, monitored carefully, can also bring forth messages.

Materials

- ✓ ½ cup of any of the following liquids: milk, lemon juice, grapefruit juice, orange juice, apple juice, sugar-water solution, clear soda such as ginger ale
- ✓ fine paintbrush
- ✓ paper
- ✓ lamp with bulb

Procedure

1. Dip brush into liquid. Write a message on paper. The message should disappear as the liquid dries.
2. To retrieve message, warm the paper over the light bulb.

Post-Activity: A fun activity would be to use deckled and aged paper (see pages 110–111) to create a treasure map!

Another Post-Activity: Consider other sources of heat to reveal the message. Would a toaster oven for 30 seconds work? How about a hairdryer?

INVISIBLE INK 2 (VEGETABLE OIL AND AMMONIA INVISIBLE INK)

[Makes 1 ½ cups]

Pre-Activity: This formula requires no heat. Many children can do the project at the same time. Just watch the ammonia.

Materials

- ✓ 1 teaspoon vegetable oil
- ✓ 5 tablespoons ammonia*
- ✓ 1 ¼ cups water
- ✓ small container
- ✓ mixing spoon
- ✓ fine art brush
- ✓ paper

The use of ammonia must be monitored carefully. Do not let children drink it, and watch that it does not splash on anyone.

Procedure

1. Mix vegetable oil and ammonia in a small container.
2. Add water carefully and stir.
3. Use the brush to write a message on the paper. The message will disappear as the fluid dries.
4. To see the message, wipe the paper with water. The message can appear and disappear quite a few times.

Post-Activity: A fun activity is to couple the invisible ink with a coded message. Create a code by moving over 1 letter in the alphabet. For example, the code letter B would stand for the real letter A. Thus, the word HELLO in code would be IFMMP. Children could have double the fun by sending a coded message in invisible ink.

INVISIBLE INK 3 (TABLE SALT INVISIBLE INK)

[Makes ¼ cup]

Pre-Activity: This method is quite safe and requires no heat. However, it needs a day for the salt solution to sufficiently dry.

Materials

- ✓ 2 tablespoons salt
- ✓ ¼ cup water
- ✓ small bowl
- ✓ mixing spoon
- ✓ fine paintbrush
- ✓ dark-colored construction paper

Procedure

1. Mix salt and water in a small bowl.
2. Dip the brush in salt-water solution and write the first letter or two of the message.
3. Dip the brush into solution again and write another few letters.
4. Keep dipping and writing until the message is complete.
5. Allow the salt solution to dry overnight. The message should appear by the next morning.

Post-Activity: A great activity with this ink would be to send a message in Morse Code AND in invisible ink. The message receiver first must reveal the invisible ink and then go back to Morse Code to reveal the words. Then the receiver could send back a message in Morse Code.

Another Post-Activity: Write the code on white paper instead of dark-colored construction paper. Rub over the area with the graphite from the pencil. The message should appear.

INVISIBLE INK 4 (WAX INVISIBLE INK)

[Makes 1]

Pre-Activity: Emergency candles can be purchased at hardware stores. Old candles without much color could be substituted. This project is an example of a resist. The wax resists the water in the watercolors.

Materials

- ✓ 1 white emergency candle or white crayons
- ✓ 1 piece white construction paper
- ✓ 1 set watercolors and paintbrush
- ✓ water

Procedure

1. Write a message on the construction paper with the candle or white crayons. The more wax used, the more successful the product will be.

2. To reveal the message, apply watercolor paints on top of paper. The wax should resist the watercolors, and the message will appear.

Post-Activity: A resist can be quite beautiful. Use the white candles to create a simple drawing, for example a seascape. Using green and blue watercolors could make the invisible ink a thing of beauty.

INVISIBLE INK 5 (BAKING SODA INVISIBLE INK)

[Makes about ¼ cup]

Pre-Activity: The grape juice concentrate contains acids. These acids react to the base in the baking soda.

Materials

- ¼ cup baking soda
- ¼ cup water
- small bowl
- mixing spoon
- ¼ cup grape juice concentrate
- 2 swabs
- paper

Procedure

1. Combine the baking soda and water in a small bowl.
2. Use a swab to write a message with the mixture on paper. Wait for the fluid to dry.
3. Swab the paper with grape juice concentrate. The message should appear.

Post-Activity: This invisible ink is an example of a chemical reaction. What other acids could substitute for the grape juice concentrate?

Cryptology Culminating Activity

Children could hide a small object somewhere that could become a treasure. Then they could create a treasure map in invisible ink on aged paper. Someone else could decode the map and find the treasure.

4 Let's Be Slimeologists!

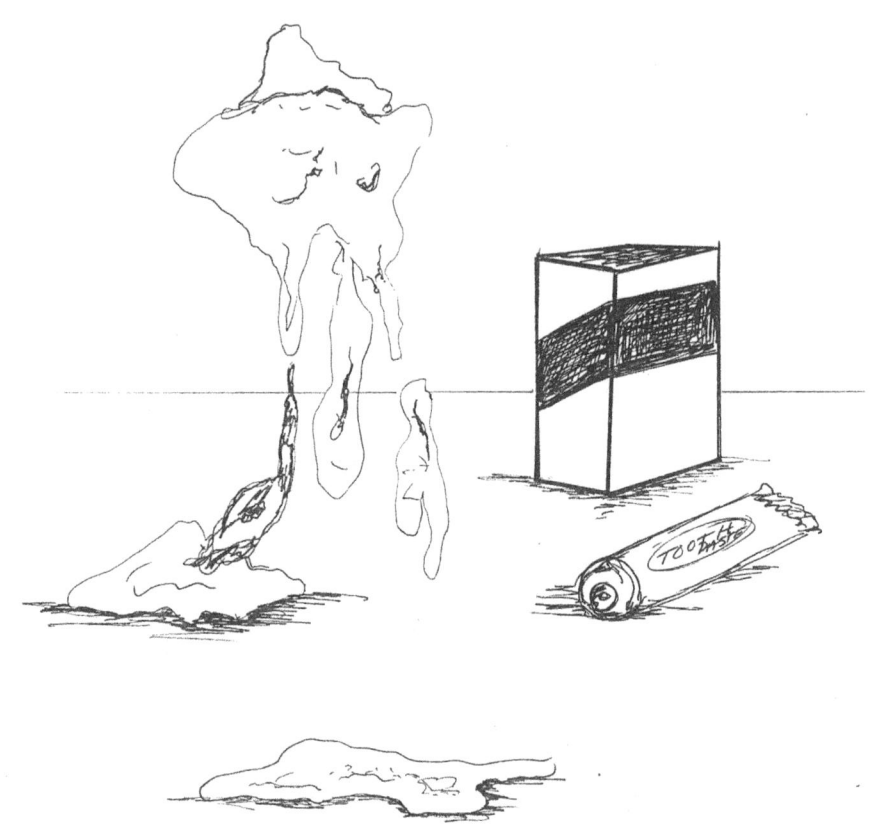

Why did I suggest we become slimeologists for this chapter? Because non-Newtonian fluidologists is quite a mouthful, and slimeologists seems much more interesting. This chapter and these activities involve fascinating non-Newtonian fluids. These fluids have properties of both solids and liquids. They resemble liquids because they take the shape of their container. They resemble solids because they can maintain a definite shape in a container much bigger than the non-Newtonian fluid. In the 1700s Isaac Newton developed a description of Newtonian fluids (substances that "behave," meaning they take the shape of their container and they flow when the container is tilted) and non-Newtonian fluids, substances that do not "behave." Ketchup is a non-Newtonian fluid because it takes the shape of the bottle, but it also retains its own shape when it is poured onto a hamburger patty. Quicksand is also a non-Newtonian fluid because it appears to be sand, but stress applied to it causes the water under the surface to quickly move the sand. Non-Newtonian fluids in this chapter can clog drains, so always dispose of the materials in a trashcan.

NON-NEWTONIAN FLUID 1 (CORNSTARCH AND WATER)

[Makes 2 cups—enough for 4 children]

Pre-Activity: Classic in its simplicity, this formula is a hit with children of all ages. In some ways this substance will act as a solid. At other times, it is a liquid. This will dry out if left exposed. It can be rejuvenated by adding a small amount of water. This is a fun activity after children read *Bartholomew and the Oobleck* by Dr. Seuss.

Materials

- 1 cup water
- 1 ½ cups cornstarch
- plastic, airtight container
- spoon

Procedure

1. Pour water into container.
2. Slowly stir in cornstarch.
3. Children really like to mix this with their hands. Then they can begin stretching and squishing.
4. Store in airtight container.

Post-Activity: For those of you who cook, you will recognize the cornstarch-water slurry as the thickening agent added to gravies, sauces, pie fillings, and more. When you use the slurry, encourage your children to watch the magic as cornstarch thickens your cooking liquid.

NON-NEWTONIAN FLUID 2 (WHITE GLUE AND LIQUID STARCH)

[Makes ¾ cup—enough for 1 child]

■ **Pre-Activity**: It snaps! It rolls! It picks up print from newspaper! It is fun!

Materials

- ½ cup white glue
- ¼ cup liquid starch
- food coloring (optional)
- spoon
- disposable container
- wax paper

Procedure

1. Mix white glue and liquid starch in disposable container.
2. Knead on wax paper until smooth.
3. If it is too sticky, add a bit more starch.
4. If it does not flow, add a bit more glue. Now children can have fun.
5. This non-Newtonian fluid does not last when stored. Use it the day you make it. Dispose in trash.

■ **Post-Activity**: Children could make a list of non-Newtonian fluids. In addition to ketchup and quicksand, toothpaste, mustard, and mayonnaise qualify.

NON-NEWTONIAN FLUID 3 (WHITE GLUE AND CONTACT LENS SOLUTION)

Pre-Activity: This activity is relatively new. Who figured out that contact lens solution had other purposes?

Materials

- 1 4-ounce bottle white glue
- ½ tablespoon baking soda
- 1 tablespoon contact lens solution
- food coloring (optional)
- disposable container
- spoon

Procedure

1. Pour all 4 ounces of white glue into disposable container.
2. Stir in baking soda.
3. Add contact lens solution and stir until mixture becomes a slime.
4. Add food coloring if desired.
5. Knead mixture and have fun!

Post-Activity: You can substitute a bottle of Elmer's Magical Liquid® for the baking soda and contact lens solution and combine it with white glue. Then you could compare the homemade recipe to the commercial product.

NON-NEWTONIAN FLUID 4 (WHITE GLUE AND BORAX)

[Makes 1 ¾ cups—enough for 3 children]

▪ **Pre-Activity**: The chemical reaction is quite thick and truly gooey. Children love it.

Materials

- ✓ 4 ounces white glue
- ✓ paper cup
- ✓ 1 ½ cups water
- ✓ plastic spoon
- ✓ 1 teaspoon borax*
- ✓ disposable container (e.g., clean butter tub)
- ✓ disposable spoon
- ✓ food coloring (optional)

Borax, as with almost all materials in this book, should not be eaten. Watch small children closely when they make this formula.

Procedure

1. Pour glue into paper cup.
2. Add ½ cup water.
3. Mix borax and the rest of the water in disposable container.
4. Carefully pour glue mixture into borax mixture and mix. Add food coloring if desired.
5. Stir. Drain off extra liquid.
6. Knead until pliable. Children can squish and squeeze.
7. Store in a plastic bag. This dries out after a great deal of use.

▪ **Post-Activity**: This activity works well with a lesson on geography. Children could create a mountain, a valley, a bluff, and so on.

NON-NEWTONIAN FLUID 5 (SCULPTING MATERIAL)

[Makes about 2 cups—enough for 2 children]

Pre-Activity: Polystyrene beads, which can be bought at craft stores, are mostly composed of air. The beads provide a substrate for the non-Newtonian fluid. Children can make sculptures from the material. Projects can dry.

Materials

- 4 ounces white glue
- paper cup
- 1 ½ cups water
- plastic spoon
- 1 teaspoon borax*
- 2 cups polystyrene beans
- large disposable container (e.g., aluminum baking pan)
- food coloring (optional)
- wax paper

Borax, as with almost all materials in this book, should not be eaten. Watch small children closely when they make this formula.

Procedure

1. Pour glue into paper cup.
2. Add ½ cup water.
3. Mix borax and rest of water in disposable container.
4. Carefully pour glue mixture into borax mixture and mix. Add food coloring if desired.
5. Slowly add polystyrene beads to mixture.
6. Remove some of the mixture and place on wax paper. Mold into desired object. Let dry on wax paper.
7. Store any remaining sculpting material in refrigerator.

Post-Activity: This material would be good for dioramas. The material could be rocks on a hill, or froth where ocean waves meet the beach, or a gravel road.

Slimeology Culminating Activity

Children could read *My Pet Slime*, written by Courtney Sheinmel and illustrated by Renée Kurilla. In the book Piper is allergic to just about every pet, so she creates a pet slime, Cosmo, and has a series of adventures. Children could write their own fictional pieces about a favorite slime.

5 Let's Be Goo-Ologists!

How are slimes different from goos? The answer is arbitrary. All the slimes in the previous chapter are non-Newtonian fluids. Goos are more Newtonian; they take the shape of their containers. However, they are still fascinating. Gelatin strings can even be eaten!

STRETCHERS

[Makes 4 tablespoons—enough for 1 child]

■ **Pre-Activity**: Children really enjoy playing with this goo, but it does have a limited lifetime.

Materials

- 2 tablespoons white glue
- food coloring (optional)
- 1 tablespoon (1 envelope) unflavored gelatin
- 2 tablespoons boiling water
- 2 small mixing bowls
- spoons
- cookie cutter
- wax paper

Procedure

1. Combine food coloring and white glue in one bowl.
2. Dissolve gelatin in boiling water in another bowl.
3. Combine the two mixtures and stir until batch thickens.
4. Place cookie cutter onto wax paper. Pour mixture into cookie cutter.
5. Allow to stand until mixture is firm.
6. Remove from cookie cutter and dry 1 hour on each side.
7. Children can now investigate their stretchers.
8. If allowed to dry, the stretchers become hard.

■ **Post-Activity**: Children could set up a system to see how far these stretchers will stretch.

FAKE PLASTIC

[Makes about 1 cup—enough for 2 children]

■ **Pre-Activity**: This wonderful material is opaque.

Materials

- ¼ cup water
- food coloring
- ¼ cup white glue
- ½ cup cornstarch
- ½ cup all-purpose flour
- kneading surface with extra flour
- 2 small mixing bowls
- mixing spoons
- wax paper

Procedure

1. Combine liquids in 1 mixing bowl.
2. Combine flour and cornstarch in the other bowl.
3. Add flour/cornstarch mixture to liquid mixture and stir until dough becomes stiff.
4. Turn mixture out onto the kneading surface (with extra flour on it) and knead for several minutes.
5. Mold creations and place on wax paper.

■ **Post-Activity**: Children could make these creations for dioramas or shadow boxes.

EPSOM SALT GOO

[Makes ¼ cup—enough for 1 child]

Pre-Activity: This goo has a unique feel! Some children at first are hesitant to knead the goo. However, that hesitation disappears quite quickly.

Materials

- 3 tablespoons white glue
- 1 ½ teaspoons Epsom salt
- 1 ½ teaspoons water
- disposable cup
- disposable spoon
- paper towels

Procedure

1. Combine Epsom salt and water in disposable cup.
2. Add white glue.
3. Stir the mixture. Pour it out on a paper towel to absorb the extra moisture.
4. Knead mixture until it becomes gooey.

Post-Activity: Because some children are sometimes reluctant to touch this goo, it is fun to make for a Halloween haunted house.

SQUEEZE GOO

[Makes about 1 ½ cups—enough for many projects]

■ **Pre-Activity**: This goo makes nice accent touches to projects. It is fun to make and use.

Materials

- 1 cup all-purpose flour
- ¼ cup salt
- ¼ cup sugar
- ¾ cup water
- food coloring
- mixing bowl
- mixing spoon
- squeeze bottle
- wax paper

Procedure

1. Combine flour, salt, and sugar in mixing bowl.
2. Add water.
3. Add drops of food coloring until the desired shade is reached.
4. Pour mixture into the squeeze bottle.
5. Squeeze goo to form designs and patterns on wax paper. It will take a day or two to dry.

■ **Post-Activity**: Finished squeeze glue creations could accent Halloween projects or Christmas scenes.

GELATIN STRINGS

[Makes about 20—enough for 10 children]

Pre-Activity: This activity actually provides a treat to eat! The gelatin is a colloid, somewhat like a liquid and somewhat like a solid.

Materials

- ✓ 1 large packet flavored gelatin
- ✓ boiling water
- ✓ cold water
- ✓ shallow pan
- ✓ plastic straws
- ✓ knife

Procedure

1. Prepare gelatin according to directions on packet.
2. Pour mixture into shallow pan and place in refrigerator for about 30 minutes. The gelatin should be thick by then.
3. Sink straws into gelatin, and place pan back into the refrigerator. Leave it there for a day.
4. The next day use the knife to cut straws out of gelatin.
5. Pinch 1 end and begin to roll up the straw so that the gelatin string pops out of the straw. Eat!

Post-Activity: Children could decide on their favorite flavor of gelatin strings. Could they add small, edible goodies, for example sprinkles, to the thickened gelatin mixture before straws are sunk?

Goo-Ology Culminating Activity

Goos are more like Newtonian fluids. Sir Isaac Newton was the first scientist to describe these fluids. Children could learn about Newton's Laws of Gravity, create some experiments, and, of course, eat some Fig Newtons.

6 Let's Be Bioscrapologists!

Some of these activities, for example growing a sweet potato vine, have been around for decades. However, in the past few years a whole new way of thinking has sprung up around the idea of growing plants from produce scraps. Now, not all these plants will produce new, delicious produce. In addition, others could take decades to provide produce. However, all these activities keep produce scraps out of landfills and provide attractive, interesting plants. Children love growing plants, and they can learn so much in the process! What conditions are necessary for growth? What kinds of plants exist? How do plants reproduce? What parts of plants do we eat? The list of possibilities goes on and on. Here are some easy ways to make growing plants from produce scraps an important part of learning.

CARROT PLANT (ROOT VEGETABLE PLANT)

[Makes 1 plant]

> **Pre-Activity**: This category of bioscrapology offers plenty of opportunities for experimentation. Any root vegetable, including radishes, horseradishes, turnips, parsnips, fennel, and beets, can be planted. Ginger can also be used. The key is to have a few leaves to start out. However, count on interesting plants but not necessarily new, edible vegetables.

Materials

- ✓ 1 carrot with green leaves and stems
- ✓ 1 plastic disposable cup
- ✓ old baking sheet
- ✓ water

Procedure

1. Cut off the top of carrot so that about an inch of it is still attached to the stem and leaves.
2. Place top in a pan of water.
3. Place baking sheet in a sunny location and keep adding water as it evaporates.
4. The new plant should begin to grow in about a week.

> **Post-Activity**: Carrots come in a variety of colors, including purple, red, white, yellow, and orange. Children could investigate whether any particular color grows the best greenery.

> **Another Post-Activity**: After growing other root vegetable plants, children could investigate which tops are edible. For example, beet greens are often featured in salads and sautés.

ROMAINE LETTUCE PLANT (BASE PLANT)

[Makes 1 plant]

Pre-Activity: Here is another large category of possible plants. What we need is the base of the lettuce and about 2 inches of stems and leaves above the base. Celery, bok choy, and red leaf lettuce all grow. What is interesting about this group is that you can harvest some of the new leaves!

Materials

- ✓ base of head of romaine lettuce with about 2 inches of leaves above the base
- ✓ 1 plastic disposable cup
- ✓ old baking sheet
- ✓ water

Procedure

1. Place base of head of romaine lettuce with 2 inches of leaves above the base in plastic, disposable cup.
2. Place cup on an old baking sheet and place baking sheet in a sunny location.
3. Water frequently.

Post-Activity: Some of the lettuces may give children some good-tasting salad ingredients.

PLANTS FROM SEEDS

> **Pre-Activity**: Perhaps this is the biggest group of bioscrapology. Just think of all the fruit seeds (apples, pears, oranges, lemons, limes, melons) and vegetable seeds (tomatoes, peppers, cucumbers, squash) that could be harvested and planted. Peaches, apricots, and nectarines have pits, meaning the seed is surrounded by a tough outer shell. To separate the seeds from the pits, carefully place each pit on its side and carefully hit the edge with a hammer. Do not hit your fingers! The pit should break apart, exposing the seed.

Materials

- ✓ seeds from fruits and vegetables
- ✓ plastic disposable glasses
- ✓ potting soil
- ✓ old baking sheet
- ✓ water

Procedure

1. Pour into the plastic disposable glasses enough potting soil to cover the bottom half of each cup.
2. Place a few seeds into each cup.
3. Cover seeds with a thin layer of soil.
4. Place the cups on an old baking sheet and place baking sheet in a sunny location.
5. Water frequently.

> **Post-Activity**: A pineapple top could also be planted in a bit of soil. No new pineapple will appear, but it will become an interesting plant all the same.

> **Another Post-Activity**: Children could prepare cherry pits for planting. Cherries need a long period of time in a very cold environment to begin germination. Clean the cherry pits and wrap them in a moist paper towel. Wrap the paper towel in aluminum foil and place the whole packet in a freezer. Check the pits after 2 months. See if they have started to germinate. If so, plant as above.

SWEET POTATO PLANT

[Makes 1 plant]

Pre-Activity: The sweet potato vine can become quite long. One year the vine went around the classroom! Children could incorporate some math into the activity by charting its weekly growth.

Materials

- ✓ 1 old sweet potato
- ✓ 4 round or square sturdy toothpicks
- ✓ 1 tall, clear plastic glass
- ✓ water

Procedure

1. Hold sweet potato so that the pointed ends are vertical. Poke 4 toothpicks into the sweet potato on all four sides of the middle.
2. Fill plastic glass with water.
3. Place one pointed end of the sweet potato into the water so that the 4 toothpicks rest on the edge of the glass. The toothpicks keep the top half out of the water. The top half of the sweet potato should remain dry, and the bottom half should be submerged in water.
4. Place the glass in a sunny spot and wait. Replace water as needed.
5. In about a week, roots will grow from the bottom, and leaves will appear from the top.
6. When the sweet potato develops vines, transplant the plant to a large pot filled with soil or to a garden.

Post-Activity: An avocado pit can be substituted for the sweet potato, although poking holes in the pit is a bit more challenging. When the plant is about 8 inches tall, cut off the top half of the leaves. This cut promotes development of new branches.

POTATO PLANT

[Makes about 5 plants, depending on the potato]

Pre-Activity: Children could find out what part of the plant the actual potato is. Children could also research types of potatoes. Finally, when harvest time comes around, they can dig up the potatoes and count how many new spuds came from 1 old spud.

Materials

- old potato with plenty of eyes
- plastic, disposable cups
- potting soil
- knife
- old baking tray

Procedure

1. Cut potato into pieces so that each piece has at least 1 eye.
2. Use knife to cut a small hole in the bottom of each cup so that extra water can drain out.
3. Pour enough potting soil into each cup to form a layer about an inch thick.
4. Place a piece of the potato in each cup and fill in with more potting soil.
5. Place the cups on the old baking tray and water. Make sure the soon-to-be plants get plenty of sun and enough but not too much water.
6. The new plants should appear within a few days. Transfer potato plants to a warm, sunny garden.

Post-Activity: Children could research various types of potatoes. What various potatoes are good for what application? They could poll friends and family about favorite potato dishes. How many potatoes are grown in the US and other countries?

Bioscrapology Culminating Activity

Children could make a large chart of plants grown, parts of plants eaten, and nutritional values. They could also decide what plants are their favorites to eat.

7 Let's Be Ornithologists!

Bird Food

Children really enjoy watching birds. They love to record types and numbers of birds, and looking for birds' nests can become a passion. Children can learn more about birds by providing bird food and by making bird feeders.

Birds can be both finicky and fickle when it comes to feeding time. For example, blue jays prefer sunflower seeds, cracked corn, and shelled peanuts. However, they will also eat doughnuts and crackers. Woodpeckers choose suet and bacon drippings, but they will also consume shelled peanuts if that is all there is.

The most popular kinds of bird food are sunflower seeds, cracked corn, suet, and niger seeds. Birds that prefer sunflower seeds seem to like the gray-striped variety best. Suet, a white, solid animal fat, can be obtained from the butcher. Place a piece of suet in a mesh bag, such as those oranges come in, or in a suet cage, and hang it from a tree branch. Niger seeds, also called thistle, are far more expensive than other kinds of seeds. Therefore, some people prefer to buy seed blends. Birds also like peanut butter and small pieces of fruits and nuts. Popped popcorn and other seeds, such as those from pumpkins, melons, and peppers, attract birds.

Many birds need grit to help grind food in their digestive tracts. One easy way to provide grit is to crush egg shells. Put clean egg shells in a plastic bag and seal. Then use a rolling pin to roll over and over the shells. It will not take long to break them up. You may also use fire ashes, sand, or commercial poultry grit.

Birds also like water, even in winter. A hose dripping into a bucket is enough to attract many winged friends.

Finally, coarse salt will bring birds. Place the grit and salt a slight distance away from the food so that birds can choose from a smorgasbord.

Once you start to feed birds, stick with the plan. Birds become accustomed to the food supply. They particularly need food in late winter and early spring.

Bird Feeders

Birds are particular about foods, and they are selective about where they eat as well. All bird feeders should be near protective bushes or trees.

Many birds (e.g., mourning doves and juncos) feed on the ground. Simply clear away fallen leaves or snow from a flat area and scatter some cracked corn.

Another way to feed birds is to make feeder trays. Place old cafeteria trays on bricks or stumps. Spread some cracked corn, breadcrumbs, or any of the above bird foods. Occasionally wash the trays.

Suet attracts many insect-eating birds such as woodpeckers. Place suet pieces in mesh bags such as those that contain produce. Garden supply stores also sell suet cages. Hang the bags or cages from tree branches.

HOMEMADE BIRD SEED MIXTURE

[Makes 4 cups]

Pre-Activity: This bird seed can be cheaper than commercial brands. It can also be tailored to specific needs. Add 3 to 5 crushed egg shells or ½ cup sand for grit.

Materials

- ✓ 1 cup black-oil sunflower seeds
- ✓ 1 ¼ cups striped sunflower seeds
- ✓ ½ cup sunflower hearts
- ✓ ½ cup millet
- ✓ ½ cup dried corn
- ✓ ¼ cup safflower seeds
- ✓ mixing bowl
- ✓ mixing spoon
- ✓ airtight container

Procedure

1. Combine all ingredients in mixing bowl.
2. Distribute to various feeders.
3. Store seed in airtight container.

Post-Activity: Children could make a favorite bird feeder, the pinecone feeder, with this mixture! Tie a piece of string about 16 inches long to the stem of a pinecone. Slather the pinecone in peanut butter, preferably chunky, and generously sprinkle bird seed mixture over, under, and around the pinecone. Shake off the excess. Tie the pinecone to a tree branch and stand back to observe.

BIRD FOOD 1 (FOOD BALLS FOR BIRDS)

[Makes 8 cups]

Pre-Activity: Because this mixture does not have to dry, children can make the bird food balls and take them outside immediately.

Materials

- 2 cups breadcrumbs
- ½ pound melted suet
- 3 chopped apples, including skin and seeds
- ½ cup all-purpose flour
- ¼ cup cornmeal
- ½ cup raisins
- ½ cup chopped nuts
- 1 cup peanut butter
- 1 cup bird seed
- mixing bowl
- mixing spoon

Procedure

1. Combine all ingredients in mixing bowl.
2. Shape into balls and put them out for birds.

Post-Activity: Children could make an easy bird feeder to hold these food balls. Take an empty, clean gallon or half-gallon plastic milk container. Cut away part of the container opposite the handle. The birds can perch on the edge of the plastic container. Place the food balls in the container. Tie the container to a junction of a tree trunk and a branch.

BIRD FOOD 2 (KABOBS FOR BIRDS)

[Makes 6]

Pre-Activity: Each kabob also provides a perch for the birds so that they can rest and eat.

Materials

- about 2 pounds of fruit pieces (such as apples, peaches, pears, or plums)
- whole grain cereals with holes (e.g., Cheerios®)
- bagel slices
- 6 pieces of string each about 30 inches long
- knife
- 6 very small disposable pie plates

Procedure

1. Use the knife to punch a small hole through the center of the bottom of each pie plate.
2. Thread the string through the bottom and make a knot. The remaining string rests in the pie plate.
3. Use the knife to make small holes in the pieces of fruit.
4. Thread the string through the fruit, cereal, and bagel slices.
5. Use the leftover string to tie the kabobs onto tree branches.

Post-Activity: Children could look around for other potential food for the kabobs. They could sprinkle bird seed on the fruit. Do birds like any cut-up and strung-up vegetables? How about no-salt crackers?

BIRDS' HOLIDAY TREE

Pre-Activity: The tradition of a birds' holiday tree goes back more than 400 years. This project is a good way for children to help the environment and have fun at the same time.

Materials

- popped, plain popcorn
- raw cranberries
- wholegrain cereal with holes (e.g., Cheerios®)
- needle and thread
- oranges, cut in half
- grapefruit, cut in half
- raisins
- sunflower seeds
- niger seeds
- small pieces of bread or crackers
- mixing bowl
- mixing spoon
- string

Procedure

1. Pick out a good tree within view of your room.
2. Make garlands from the thread, popcorn, cranberries, and cereal. Hang garlands from the tree.
3. Scoop out pulp from oranges and grapefruit. Mix the pulp with raisins, sunflower seeds, niger seeds, and small pieces of bread or crackers.
4. Spoon a bit of the pulp mixture back into each orange or grapefruit half. Attach strings to the shell and hang shells from the tree.

Post-Activity: While this activity is traditionally tied to Christmas, the birds could gain sustenance from the tree at other times, for example Thanksgiving, and particularly Easter. Sometimes very little is available to birds in early springtime and Easter. Since we are on a roll, how about a Fourth of July tree, with peaches, blueberries, and strawberries?

HUMMINGBIRD BREW

[Makes 4 cups]

> **Pre-Activity**: To first attract hummingbirds, make a 1 to 3 ratio of sugar to water. After the hummingbirds become regular customers, change the ratio to 1 to 4. Wash the hummingbird feeder every week. Hummingbirds are attracted to the color red. Make sure some portion of the hummingbird feeder is bright red.

Materials

- ✓ 1 cup sugar
- ✓ 4 cups water
- ✓ stove or heating element
- ✓ pot
- ✓ hummingbird feeder, at least partially red

Procedure

1. Combine sugar and water in pot and boil for 2 minutes.
2. Let solution cool and pour into hummingbird feeder.

> **Post-Activity**: Hummingbirds are particular about their feeders. Children could investigate the best location. Hummers do not like their feeders to be near other bird feeders, and they prefer to be within 10 feet of trees and shrubs.

Ornithology Culminating Activity

John James Audubon, born in 1785, was both an artist and an ornithologist. He spent a good portion of his life painting bird species. He printed a very famous collection of these bird illustrations in *The Birds of America*. The book consisted of 435 pages of over 700 species of American birds. Children could also be both artists and ornithologists and paint some illustrations of the birds they see visiting the bird feeders. They could use paints from Chapter 15 on chromatology.

8 Let's Be Entomologists!

Entomology is the study of insects. While we try to get rid of certain insects, for example mosquitoes, we want to encourage beneficial insects to visit our outdoor spaces. The following activities increase children's knowledge of insects and help our environment as well. An activity about worms has been included here. Technically, entomologists study only insects, and worms do not have six legs. However, we can be a little loose in our studies.

FOOD FOR ALL KINDS OF BUGS

[Makes 1 cup—enough for about 3 days]

Pre-Activity: This food attracts bees and wasps as well as butterflies and ants. Therefore, children must watch out for stinging insects.

Materials

✓ 1 cup over-ripe fruit, cut into pieces

✓ 1 small, disposable pie pan

Procedure

1. Place the over-ripe fruit in the disposable pie pan.
2. Put the pie pan on a rock or large piece of wood. Give your insect guests time to find it.

Post-Activity: Insects are attracted to rotting fruit. Children could see which fruit insects seem to seek. Children could see if certain insects like certain fruits. Math and graphing could be incorporated here.

MOTH ATTRACTOR GOO

[Makes 1 batch]

Pre-Activity: Moths are for the most part night insects. The attractor goo can be prepared during the day, but a night visit is essential to see the moths.

Materials

- ✓ 2 cups orange juice that has been at room temperature for about 2 days
- ✓ 4 over-ripe bananas
- ✓ ½ cup honey or corn syrup
- ✓ mixing bowl
- ✓ mixing spoon
- ✓ plastic wrap
- ✓ old paintbrush
- ✓ flashlight

Procedure

1. Place peeled bananas in the bowl and mash with the back of the mixing spoon.
2. Add orange juice and combine.
3. Add honey or corn syrup and combine.
4. Cover bowl with plastic wrap and allow it to sit outside in the sun for several hours.
5. Take the mixture and an old paintbrush to a clearing where several trees are next to open space.
6. Paint several tree trunks with the mixture.
7. After dark, return to the area and see if the moths like the mixture.

Post-Activity: Children could see if other types of animals, for example squirrels or chipmunks, also like the mixture.

Another Post-Activity: Children could learn more about butterflies and moths. Then they could make a Venn diagram regarding moths and butterflies.

BUTTERFLY BREW

[Makes 1 quart—enough for 1 feeder for about 3 weeks]

Pre-Activity: Butterflies seek out nectar from flowers. This brew satisfies their taste buds as well. Butterflies are attracted to bright colors, especially orange and purple. Therefore, color the butterfly feeder (nectar container) bright orange and purple. Clean the container often so that the nectar does not spoil.

Materials

- 1 quart water
- 1 cup sugar
- old pot
- stove or heating element
- mixing spoon
- small, empty, clean cottage cheese container
- sponge cut to the size of the cottage cheese container (hopefully painted orange or purple)
- airtight container

Procedure

1. Pour water into the pot and heat until it boils.
2. Turn down heat and add sugar. Stir and cook until all the sugar is dissolved.
3. Remove pot from the heat and allow solution to cool.
4. Place sponge in empty cottage cheese container.
5. Pour in enough nectar to more than cover sponge.
6. Place the container on a rock or ledge in a sunny part of the garden. Wait for your guests!
7. Refrigerate remaining nectar in airtight container.
8. Replace nectar every 3–4 days.

Post-Activity: Children could see if butterflies visit during special times of the day.

Another Post-Activity: Children could read *The Very Hungry Caterpillar* by Eric Carle. At the end the caterpillar has turned into a beautiful butterfly. Children could draw and color another beautiful butterfly. Let's take this project one step further; butterflies are symmetrical. Children could check to see if the butterflies they drew are symmetrical.

LADYBUG HOTEL

[Makes 1]

Pre-Activity: Many insects, such as ladybugs and praying mantises, help our environment by eating not-so-beneficial bugs. All the beneficial bugs need a place to stay.

Materials

- ✓ 1 empty, clean gallon milk container
- ✓ scissors
- ✓ toilet paper tubes
- ✓ organic materials, such as hollow twigs, dead leaves, pinecones, pine needles, and straw

Procedure

1. Cut away the side of milk carton opposite the handle.
2. Place toilet paper tubes on the floor of the milk carton so that the hollow portions face out.
3. Fill tubes with dead leaves, pine needles, and straw.
4. Place hollow twigs inside milk carton so that again the hollow portion faces out.
5. Add other organic matter above the hollow twigs.
6. Place ladybug hotel in a shady spot in a garden where there is not much wind.
7. Your hotel will not be occupied for a while, but hopefully bugs will find it.
8. Make sure hotel stays dry and clean. At the end of fall, remove all the contents.

Post-Activity: Children could make a list of the insects that come for a stay.

Another Post-Activity: Children could paint the hotel by using the Versatile Paint formula (see page 95). They could give the hotel a name and decorate the milk container with their own stickers (see page 123).

WORM FARM

[Makes 1]

> **Pre-Activity**: Entomologists study six-legged creatures, so they do not study worms. However, worms are so beneficial to our soil and so interesting that we like to study them. A worm farm is a great way to both study worms and help our gardens and environment. Worm poop, called castings, is rich in organic matter that fertilizes the soil. Also, worms create tunnels through soil, thus aerating and improving the soil. By the way, the intentional raising of worms is called vermiculture; we are therefore vermiculturists. Worms are strict vegetarians, so do not include any meat or dairy products in the produce scraps.

Materials

- ✓ 2 buckets, 1 must have a lid
- ✓ drill and 3/8 bit
- ✓ soil
- ✓ rock or other solid object about 2 inches by 2 inches by 2 inches
- ✓ organic matter such as dead leaves, small twigs, or pine needles, etc.
- ✓ chopped up produce scraps such as banana peels, greens, apple peels, tea leaves, etc.
- ✓ water
- ✓ worms (can be purchased at bait shops, convenience stores, even the Internet)

Procedure

1. Use the drill and bit to make holes in the bottom of 1 of the buckets. Also drill holes in the lid.
2. Place the rock in the bottom of the bucket that does not have holes in it. The purpose of the rock is to create space between the 2 buckets and thus to allow water a place to go.
3. Place the bucket with holes on top of the rock and into the other bucket so that any extra moisture will enter the bottom bucket.
4. Add a layer of soil to the bucket that has holes in the bottom. Top with a layer of organic matter and chopped-up produce scraps. Add a thin layer of sand on top. Moisten with water so that the surface feels like a wrung-out sponge.
5. Repeat the layers, moistening each layer, until the bucket is about ¾ full. Top with a final layer of soil. Again moisten.
6. Count your worms and gently add them to the bucket.
7. Top with the lid that has holes in it. The holes provide air circulation. Worms need fresh air.

8. Every few days add more organic matter and food scraps. Worms eat a lot! Moisten the bucket contents.

9. Worms double their population every 60 days. After 60 days gently find your worms and count. What is your new worm population?

10. Worm poop, called castings, is rich in organic matter. Occasionally, remove the rich composting and add it to gardens or forests. Start your worm farm over again!

Post-Activity: Children could track the number of worms in their worm farm. Does the population really double in 60 days? They could record what happens to the organic matter and produce scraps.

Entomology Culminating Activity

Using the above activities, children have created a restaurant for various types of insects and worms. They could create a name for their restaurant and compose an elaborate menu with all the options.

9 Let's Be Vulcanologists!

Vulcanologists study volcanoes and volcanic eruptions. Beneath the earth's solid crust, molten rock, also called magma, is lighter than solid rock. The lighter magma tries to rise to the earth's surface. When the less dense, very hot magma finds a fissure to the earth's surface, a volcanic eruption occurs. Then the magma becomes lava. The lava cools down to become igneous rock, becoming part of the rock cycle. Four main types of volcanic eruption are studied; some lava flows easily while other eruptions are quite explosive. All four types are presented here.

VOLCANO MODEL

[Makes 3 ½ cups—enough for 1 map]

Pre-Activity: A volcano must be created before it can erupt. This volcano is a version of a salt map. It will take a couple of days to dry. However, it can last for years. Alum, found in the spice section of a grocery store, helps this mixture dry fairly quickly. The dough is not grainy and can be rolled to make coils. The coils can then be shaped to wrap around the yogurt container to form the volcano. More mixture can be added to make the volcano realistic. Paints can be added during the mixing instead of after the map has dried. See Versatile Paint formula on page 95.

Materials

- ✓ 1 cup salt
- ✓ 2 cups all-purpose flour
- ✓ 2 teaspoons alum
- ✓ approximately 1 cup water
- ✓ mixing bowl
- ✓ mixing spoon
- ✓ empty, clean yogurt container
- ✓ old baking sheet
- ✓ paints and paintbrushes

Procedure

1. Mix salt, flour, and alum together in the bowl.
2. Add enough water, slowly and in small amounts, to make stiff dough.
3. Place yogurt container in middle of old baking sheet.
4. Form some dough into coils and surround the yogurt container.
5. Smooth out coils to form the sides of the volcano. Add more mixture to make the volcano look realistic.
6. Paint when thoroughly dry (1–2 days).

Post-Activity: This recipe is an adaptation of a salt map mixture. Salt map activities have been around for decades. The ratio between salt and flour gives finished products different textures. Children could make small amounts of the recipe above but add much more salt. What is the result?

VOLCANIC ACTION 1 (STROMBOLIAN ERUPTION)

[Makes 1]

Pre-Activity: Stromboli is an island near Sicily. Its volcano, rising more than 3,000 feet above sea level, has been active for several millennia. It can erupt constantly for periods of up to several years. Strombolian eruptions are seldom violent; lava and gases flow easily and are not pent up. In this experiment, the action is quick, producing an abundance of small bubbles.

Materials

- ✓ 1 volcano model (see previous page)
- ✓ 1 tablespoon baking soda
- ✓ 1 cup white vinegar
- ✓ red and green food coloring (optional)

Procedure

1. Pour baking soda into the volcano model's yogurt container.
2. Mix vinegar with food colorings (optional).
3. Pour vinegar into yogurt container. Very quickly the baking soda and vinegar will produce carbon dioxide, causing the volcano to erupt.

Post-Activity: In this experiment, the vinegar, an acid, reacts with the baking soda, a base. Children could try other acids, such as lemon juice or lime juice, to see how the results differ.

VOLCANIC ACTION 2 (HAWAIIAN ERUPTION)

[Makes 1]

Pre-Activity: Hawaiian eruptions, named after the Hawaiian volcanoes, are somewhat predictable. The lava often exits from several vents. Hawaiian eruptions are the least violent. The dishwashing liquid slows the eruption of this volcano, producing a cascading liquid that keeps its shape longer than the previous formula.

Materials

- ✓ 1 volcano model (see above)
- ✓ 1 tablespoon baking soda
- ✓ 1 teaspoon dishwashing liquid
- ✓ 1 cup white vinegar
- ✓ red and green food coloring (optional)

Procedure

1. Pour baking soda and dishwashing liquid into the volcano model's yogurt container.
2. Mix vinegar with food colorings (optional).
3. Pour vinegar into the volcano model's yogurt container.
4. The dishwashing liquid delays contact between baking soda and vinegar. The overall reaction is longer and not so vigorously "volcanic" as the Strombolian eruption.

Post-Activity: Children could experiment with different types of dish soap to see what gives the best results.

VOLCANIC ACTION 3 (VULCANIAN ERUPTION)

[Makes 1]

Pre-Activity: Vulcanian eruptions get their name from Vulcano, an island near Italy. Inside this type of volcano, thick magma builds up inside a central vent. Ultimately, gases increase pressure under the magma, and the magma explodes into dust and large pieces of debris. Effervescent antacid tablets contain, among other ingredients, sodium bicarbonate (baking soda) and citric acid. The addition of extra baking soda just keeps the process going longer. Although the volcanic reaction in this activity is not as fast as the Strombolian eruption, the results are more explosive.

Materials

- ✓ 1 volcano model (see above)
- ✓ 2 effervescent antacid tablets (e.g., Alka-Seltzer®)
- ✓ 1 teaspoon baking soda
- ✓ red and green food coloring (optional)
- ✓ ½ cup water

Procedure

1. Place antacid tablets, baking soda, and food coloring (optional) into the volcano model's yogurt container.
2. Add water. Watch the effects.

Post-Activity: Children could research how antacid tablets help people feel better.

VOLCANIC ACTION 4 (PELÉAN ERUPTION)

[Makes 1]

Pre-Activity: In 1902, Mount Pelée on the Caribbean island Martinique erupted, killing more than 35,000 people. Peléan eruptions, named after Mount Pelée, are the most violent types of volcanic eruptions. The thick magma and gases clog a central vent in the volcano. Pressure builds until a terrifying explosion occurs—hot ash and dust cloud the atmosphere. Often, parts of the mountain portion of the volcano are destroyed. In this activity the yeast acts as a catalyst and breaks down the hydrogen peroxide into water and oxygen. The oxygen is caught by the dish soap, and large and long-lasting bubbles appear. This is a favorite with children.

Materials

- ✓ 1 volcano model (see above)
- ✓ 1 tablespoon yeast (1 packet) mixed with 3 tablespoons warm water
- ✓ 1 teaspoon dish soap
- ✓ ½ cup hydrogen peroxide
- ✓ food coloring (optional)

Procedure

1. Pour hydrogen peroxide and dish soap into volcano model's yogurt container.
2. Add food coloring if desired.
3. Quickly add yeast-water mixture.
4. Large, rolling bubbles appear.

Post-Activity: This activity is exothermic; heat is produced. The yogurt container gets warm but not hot. Since the yogurt container is surrounded by salt map material, children cannot feel the heat. If you repeat the experiment using a different disposable container, children can feel the warmth.

Vulcanology Culminating Activity

Children could mark on a large map the locations of current and past active volcanoes. They will find that most eruptions have occurred around the edges of the Pacific Ocean. This border is called the Ring of Fire. Children could research why this ring exists. They could also learn about hotspot volcanoes.

10 Let's Be Paleontologists!

Paleontologists study ancient life. Some people believe paleontologists study only dinosaurs. However, these scientists also study all other early life, including plants, invertebrates, vertebrates, and even microbes. They learn about these ancient living things by studying various types of fossils. Children learn about 5 different types of fossils in the following activities.

For years I used plaster of Paris to make these fossils. However, today experts feel plaster of Paris could cause health concerns for children. Therefore, other recipes have been substituted. The results are not quite the same.

MOLD AND CAST FOSSIL

[Makes 2 cups—enough for 1 demonstration]

Pre-Activity: A cast fossil of an organism is usually not the real organism. Millions of years ago an animal fell into a clay-like substance and died. Over time the animal disintegrated, leaving an impression, called a mold, in the clay-like material. Water containing dissolved minerals entered the mold over thousands of years. Eventually the water seeped out but the minerals remained, filling the mold. The minerals, forming a cast, hardened into the shape of the original organism.

Materials to make the mold

- ✓ 1 cup baking soda
- ✓ ½ cup cornstarch
- ✓ ⅔ cup warm water
- ✓ pot
- ✓ stove or heating element
- ✓ mixing spoon
- ✓ food coloring (optional)
- ✓ bone, seashell, or twig

Procedure to make the mold

1. Stir together baking soda and cornstarch in pot.
2. Add warm water and stir. Heat on medium heat until it boils. It will look like mashed potatoes.
3. Remove from stove and cool.
4. Knead clay and add food coloring if desired.
5. Form into a land feature that looks like the side of a riverbed.
6. While the clay is still soft, press the real bone, shell, or twig into the clay in 2 different locations. Remove the real object. You now have made 2 molds of the real object. You will leave 1 mold empty.

Materials to make the cast

- ✓ 1 batch Squeeze Goo from Goo-Ology chapter (see page 31)

Procedure to make the cast

1. Fill 1 mold with Squeeze Goo. The cast will harden in a day or 2.
2. Leave the other mold empty.
3. Now the mold and cast fossil is complete!

Post-Activity: Children could mold various objects and compare results. Hopefully children could even learn from the mold what the original organism looked like.

TRACE FOSSIL (DINOSAUR FOOTPRINTS)

[Makes 4 footprints]

Pre-Activity: A fossil can be broadly defined as a hardened trace of an animal or plant. A dinosaur's footprint is a type of trace fossil.

Materials

- ✓ 1 batch of mold dough from mold and cast activity (see page 61)
- ✓ petroleum jelly
- ✓ plastic replica of a dinosaur with distinctive feet
- ✓ wax paper

Procedure

1. Coat dinosaur replica's feet with petroleum jelly. The petroleum jelly will keep the mold dough from sticking to the dinosaur replica.
2. Pour mold dough onto wax paper and smooth it out to look like a land feature.
3. Have dinosaur replica "step" into and out of mold dough. The replica should have left footprints.
4. Let the mold dough harden overnight. The next day examine the footprints.

Post-Activity: Children could use this activity to explore other animals' footprints. They could conclude that small animal footprints mean small animals. They could also investigate bird footprints and carve those footprints into the dough. Examples would be duck footprints and eagle talon prints.

Another Post-Activity: Children could measure their stride distance, the distance between a left and right foot while walking. Then they could conclude that small children have shorter stride distances that tall children. They could then research what paleontologists learn from dinosaur footprints and their strides.

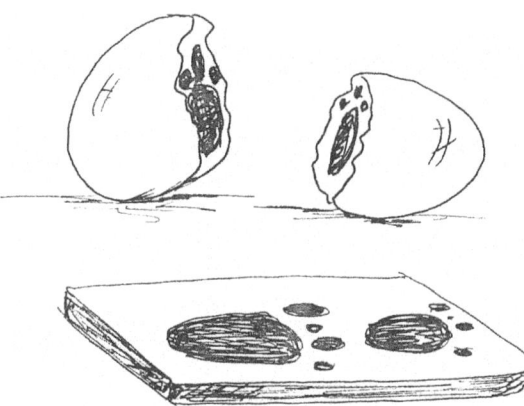

CARBON FILM FOSSIL

[Makes 3 imprints]

Pre-Activity: During prehistoric times some organisms, particularly plants, were sandwiched between layers of earth, pressing and heating the organism's remains. Over time the organism's fluids and gases were forced out of the remains. Since all organisms are carbon-based, a thin film of carbon remained, forming a carbon film fossil.

Materials

- ✓ fresh but sturdy leaves or flowers
- ✓ paints (see Chapter 15 on chromatology) and paintbrush
- ✓ 1 batch of mold dough from mold and cast activity (see page 61)
- ✓ wax paper

Procedure

1. Spoon mold dough onto wax paper and smooth dough out until it looks like a land feature.
2. Paint one side of the leaf or flower being fossilized.
3. Press the fresh leaf or flower into plaster with painted side down. Carefully remove. A carbon film imprint in the plaster should remain. Add further details with paint if you wish.
4. Let the mold dough harden overnight. The next day examine the imprint.

Post-Activity: Children could try various combinations of different clays and doughs, different paints, and different plants or flowers to create several different carbon film fossils.

FOSSIL EGGS

[Makes 4 eggs]

> **Pre-Activity**: Another type of fossil is the egg fossil. Sometimes floods or other geographic tragedies engulfed and thus preserved dinosaur eggs.

Materials

- ✓ 4 plastic break-apart eggs that are sold during Easter
- ✓ petroleum jelly
- ✓ 1 empty egg carton
- ✓ ½ cup white glue
- ✓ ½ cup shampoo
- ✓ 1 ½ cups all-purpose flour
- ✓ mixing bowl
- ✓ mixing spoon
- ✓ paints (see Chapter 15 on chromatology) and paintbrush

Procedure

1. Break apart the plastic eggs. Coat the insides of the plastic eggs with petroleum jelly.
2. Place the egg halves in the empty egg carton.
3. Combine white glue, shampoo, and flour in mixing bowl.
4. Spoon dough into each plastic egg half.
5. Combine the plastic egg halves together, making whole eggs.
6. Let "eggs" age for a day or two.
7. Remove plastic egg halves, leaving solid fossil eggs.
8. Paint.

> **Post-Activity**: Children could make bird eggs instead of fossil eggs and paint, referencing a bird book. They could also make a few broken eggs that are mostly empty to show baby birds are born and no longer need the egg shells.

AMBER WITH INCLUSIONS

[Makes 1]

> **Pre-Activity**: Amber is fossilized resin from prehistoric trees. Sometimes bits of life were included in the liquid resin before it became solid. These bits might be insects, flowers, leaves, fur, hair, and even larger life, including frogs and pieces of wood. Before you start this activity, decide on your inclusion. This amber gels very quickly! It is fun!

Materials

- ¼ teaspoon borax*
- ½ cup warm water in disposable cup
- red and yellow food colorings
- ½ cup clear glue
- ½ cup water in another disposable but transparent cup
- old spoon
- your inclusion (flower, small piece of wood, plastic insect, etc.)

Borax, as with almost all materials in this book, should not be eaten. Watch small children closely when they make this formula.

Procedure

1. Pour borax into warm water in the disposable cup. Stir to combine.
2. Add 2 drops of red food coloring and 2 drops of yellow food coloring to the warm water. Stir. The water should now be a lovely orange color. Add more of one color to perfect your version of orange.
3. Add the clear glue into the water in the other disposable but transparent cup and stir.
4. Now the magic happens! Add a small amount of the borax solution into the water-glue solution and stir. The mixture will start to gel.
5. Place your inclusion into the water-glue cup and add the rest of the borax mixture. Stir to combine all ingredients and enclose your inclusion.
6. Let sit for a couple of hours until your amber is solid.

Post-Activity: Children could make several color ambers with several different inclusions.

Fossil Culminating Activity

Children could create a museum display of all their fossils. They could paint a background on oaktag, include dinosaur replicas, and provide comment cards for each fossil.

11 Let's Be Hydrologists!

Water is essential to our lives, and hydrologists study water and its relation to Earth. Water has amazing properties; it is both adhesive and cohesive. It is a key element of clouds and all sorts of precipitation. All plants and animals need water to survival. Water provides a home to both freshwater and saltwater organisms. Finally, it is called the universal solvent because it dissolves many, many other substances.

AMAZING WATER 1 (DEMONSTRATION OF ADHESION AND COHESION)

[Makes 1 demonstration]

Pre-Activity: Water molecules like to stick to each other (cohesion). Water molecules also like to cling to other substances (adhesion). This experiment takes some practice; children might want to conduct this experiment outside.

Materials

- large measuring cup with pouring spout
- another smaller glass container
- water
- food coloring
- piece of string about 36 inches long

Procedure

1. Fill measuring cup with water.
2. Add enough food coloring to make liquid very visible.
3. Soak string for about 30 seconds in water.
4. Tie 1 end of the string to the measuring cup handle and pull the string across the spout.
5. The other end of the string should be in the smaller glass container.
6. Hold the measuring cup in one hand and the string in the smaller glass container in the other hand.
7. Stretch the string as far as it will go and raise the measuring cup about 1 foot higher than the smaller glass container.
8. Slowly pour the liquid from the measuring cup.
9. Hopefully the liquid follows along the string and fills the smaller glass container. This takes some practice.

Post-Activity: The activity calls for soaking the string. What would happen if the string is dry?

AMAZING WATER 2 (ANOTHER DEMONSTRATION OF ADHESION AND COHESION)

[Makes 1 demonstration]

Pre-Activity: This experiment is dramatic because water sticks to itself (cohesion) and sticks to the walls of the glass (adhesion).

Materials

- small glass
- water
- medicine dropper
- several drops of food coloring
- container larger than glass

Procedure

1. Place the glass in the container. The container will catch the overflow.
2. Almost fill the glass with water.
3. Add several drops of food coloring to the water. The food coloring will aid in seeing the properties of adhesion and cohesion.
4. Now carefully fill the medicine dropper with more water. Drop the water onto the surface of the water. Do not touch the surface with the dropper.
5. Look across the surface of the water as more and more water drops are dropped onto the surface. A visible dome, highlighted by the food coloring, will become apparent.
6. Keep dropping water. The height of the dome will become amazing! Eventually the adhesion and cohesion forces fail, and water spills into the larger container.

Post-Activity: This activity could easily involve math. How many drops of water can be dropped before one drop is one drop too many? Does a wider glass influence results? Would adding something like salt or sugar change what happens?

OCEAN IN A BOTTLE

[Makes 1]

Pre-Activity: The "ocean" is caused by the fact that oil and water do not mix. Mineral oil can be purchased at a pharmacy.

Materials

- ✓ 1 empty, clear plastic 1-liter bottle with lid
- ✓ 1 ½ cups mineral oil
- ✓ small bowl
- ✓ water
- ✓ several drops blue food coloring
- ✓ masking tape

Procedure

1. Pour mineral oil into bottle.
2. Mix water and food coloring in bowl.
3. Pour enough blue water into bottle to fill it.
4. Screw on the lid and seal with tape.
5. Turn the bottle on its side and rock gently to watch the "ocean."

Post-Activity: Children could research the relationship between oceans, tides, waves, and the moon.

HOMEMADE CLOUD

[Makes 1]

Pre-Activity: Clouds form when water vapor, which is invisible, turns into small water droplets.

Materials

- ✓ 3 cups very hot water
- ✓ 4-cup heat-resistant glass measuring cup (e.g., Pyrex®)
- ✓ piece of cheesecloth big enough to cover top of measuring cup
- ✓ rubber band large enough to go around top of measuring cup
- ✓ 10 ice cubes

Procedure

1. Pour hot water into the measuring cup.
2. Carefully touch the side of the measuring cup. When measuring cup becomes fairly hot, pour out all but about ½ cup of the water.
3. Cover the top of the measuring cup with the cheesecloth.
4. Fasten rubber band around the cheesecloth and the top of the measuring cup.
5. Place ice cubes on top of cheesecloth.
6. Water vapor will form small clouds.

Post-Activity: Children could make a table with types of clouds (cirrus, cumulus, stratus) and describe them or draw pictures of them. They could find out which types produce precipitation.

LAYERS OF LIQUID

[Makes 1]

Pre-Activity: Children could hypothesize about why this demonstration works. What would happen if they prepared another jar and put the honey in last?

Materials

- ½ cup honey or syrup
- ½ cup water
- several drops red food coloring
- ½ cup vegetable oil
- clear plastic pint jar
- small bowl
- spoon

Procedure

1. Pour honey into jar.
2. Combine food coloring and water in small bowl.
3. Pour food coloring/water mixture slowly on top of the honey. To slow down the process, place the spoon in the jar and trickle the water against the back of the spoon. The water should stay on top of the honey.
4. Slowly trickle the vegetable oil on top of the water. Children could record their observations.

Post-Activity: Water and oil do not mix well. Children could investigate other fluids that might replicate this experiment. They will find that juices, vinegars, and milks are mostly all water and should be good substitutes for plain water.

Hydrology Culminating Activity

Children have now found out how important water is to all organisms, including people. They could write a poem, praising and thanking water for all that it does for the earth.

12 Let's Be Musicologists!

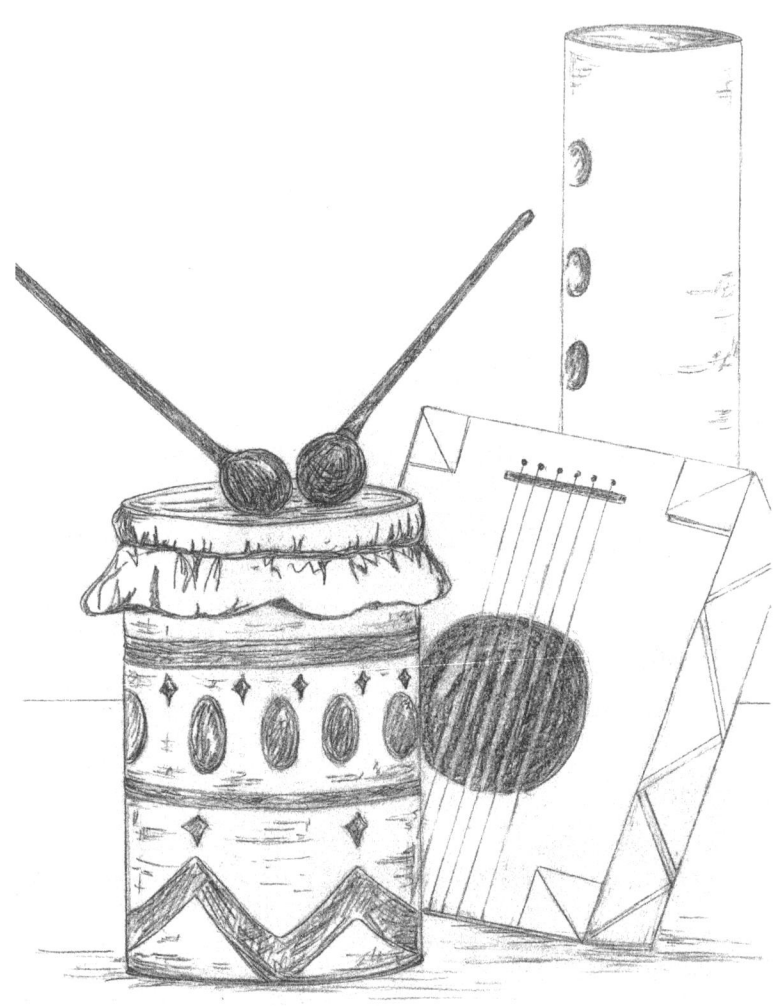

Musicologists study the history and science of music. Music is made when an instrument (or voice) vibrates, making waves. Those waves travel through air by transferring vibrations from molecule to molecule, carrying sound. We hear the music when the waves vibrate against our eardrums. We create music in various ways, including blowing through a tube (e.g., a trumpet), vibrating strings (e.g., a violin) or hitting something (e.g., a drum). Children could create all kinds of instruments simply by examining items around the house, particularly in the kitchen. They can look for items to gently tap or gently blow. Children learn a great deal about music when they make their own instruments, and they also learn about the science of sound.

WATER GLASS MUSICAL INSTRUMENTS

[Makes 1 set]

Pre-Activity: Children could note that the more the water, the lower the sound.

Materials

- ✓ 8 glasses, each at least 6 inches tall
- ✓ ruler
- ✓ water
- ✓ metal spoon

Procedure

1. Line up 8 glasses.
2. Fill first glass to the top with water to produce the low C note.
3. Use ruler to fill the next glass 8/9 full to produce the D note.
4. Use ruler to fill the next glass 4/5 full to produce the E note.
5. Fill next glass ¾ full to produce the F note.
6. Fill next glass ⅔ full to produce the G note.
7. Use ruler to fill the next glass 3/5 full to produce the A note.
8. Fill next glass 8/15 full to produce the B note.
9. Fill last glass halfway to produce the high C note.
10. Gently tap each glass with metal spoon and begin to make music.

Post-Activity: Children could play some simple melodies, like "Twinkle, Twinkle, Little Star" or "Happy Birthday."

Another Post-Activity: Children could tap the glasses with something other than a metal spoon, for example a wooden spoon or the handle of a silicone spatula. What happens to the sound?

KAZOO

[Makes 1]

Pre-Activity: Music is created when the humming causes the wax paper to vibrate. Children could decorate the tubing with markers, paint, or their own handmade stickers (see page 123).

Materials

- ✓ 1 cardboard tube from paper towels
- ✓ 1 sheet wax paper about 8 inches by 8 inches
- ✓ 1 rubber band
- ✓ 1 sharpened pencil

Procedure

1. Place wax paper over one end of tube and fasten with the rubber band. Make sure wax paper is flat over the opening.
2. With pencil point, make a small puncture in the tube about 2 inches from the wax paper end.
3. To play, hum through the open end of the kazoo. See what happens when the hole is covered.

Post-Activity: This activity lends itself to a kazoo marching band.

TAMBOURINES

[Makes 2]

Pre-Activity: Children could try different fillings inside the paper plates. Can different sounds be made? Children could also decorate the plates prior to sealing them together.

Materials

- ✓ 4 paper plates
- ✓ about ½ cup dried large beans, beads, or uncooked pasta
- ✓ masking tape

Procedure

1. Place 2 plates up on the table.
2. Pour about ¼ cup beans, beads, or uncooked pasta into each plate.
3. Cover each plate with another plate so that the rims touch.
4. Completely seal the edges together with tape.
5. Shake or hit tambourines to make music.

Post-Activity: Children could make a different type of tambourine, a wood stick tambourine. They could loosely nail bottle caps to a strip of wood about 2 inches by 2 inches by 9 inches. Play the wood stick tambourine by shaking it or by gently striking it against another surface.

RUBBER BAND GUITAR

[Makes 1]

Pre-Activity: The frame for the rubber bands must be very sturdy. Children can investigate how different rubber bands can produce different pitches.

Materials

- ✓ 1 square metal tin about 6 inches by 6 inches (no lid is necessary)
- ✓ about 6 big rubber bands of varying widths

Procedure

1. Place the rubber bands around the top and bottom of the metal tin. Make sure the rubber bands are parallel to each other.
2. Twang away!

Post-Activity: Children could make guitars from a variety of different boxes, including boxes made of wood or plastic. They can also see how sound changes by using different types and widths of rubber bands.

STEEL DRUMS

[Makes 1 set]

Pre-Activity: Real steel drums, popular in the Caribbean region, are made from cut oil drums that are pounded and tuned. Empty food tins can be substituted for the steel drums. Small tins make high notes, and big tins make low notes.

Materials

- ✓ 3 empty, clean food tins (cookie or popcorn tins work well)
- ✓ 2 unsharpened pencils
- ✓ about 6 rubber bands

Procedure

1. The empty food tins become the drums. The tins could be painted or covered with pretty decorations.
2. Wrap the rubber bands around the unsharpened pencils to make the drumsticks.
3. Hit inside of tins with drumsticks. Have a good time!

Post-Activity: Children can make other types of drums. A very simple one is an empty oatmeal canister. They can hit the lid with drumsticks as above, or they can play the drum bongo-style. They can try various other containers, such as plastic bins or cardboard boxes. They can record how sounds change as different size containers become drums. Children could also explore how sound changes if the containers are not empty.

Musicology Culminating Activity

Children could create a band with all the instruments. They could also create an original piece of music and perform it.

13 Let's Be Time Travelers!

In this chapter we are traveling back to colonial times. In 1776, about 96 percent of adults were farmers. Today about 4 percent of adults are farmers. Our society has certainly become very specialized, and daily life is very different from that of the colonial period. Hopefully these activities will help children see how colonial people lived. Toys were precious and usually homemade. Frankly, colonial children were often busy with chores and did not have as much play time as today's children have.

YARN DOLLS

[Makes 1]

Pre-Activity: Colonial children had few toys, and toys were made from what was available. Yarn dolls were made of leftover bits of yarn from other projects.

Materials

- ✓ about 10 yards yarn
- ✓ cardboard scrap about 8 inches wide
- ✓ scissors

Procedure

1. Wind the yarn around the cardboard at least 16 times and cut at the end of the last wind.
2. Cut 7 more pieces of yarn about 10 inches each.
3. Cut yarn at bottom of the cardboard and remove cardboard.
4. Tie 1 piece of the 10-inch yarn around the yarn strands about 1 inch from the top to form the head.
5. Pull away 8 strands of yarn from the body to form an arm. Tie with a 10-inch piece of yarn to form a shoulder. Cut some of the yarn off so that the arm is not too long. Tie with a piece of the 10-inch yarn.
6. Repeat for the other arm.
7. With another piece of 10-inch yarn, tie the remaining 16 pieces to form a waist.
8. For a girl doll, trim the yarn to form the bottom of the skirt.
9. For a boy doll, pull away 8 strands and tie at the ankle with one 10-inch piece of yarn.
10. Repeat for the other leg.

Post-Activity: Children could make beds from small boxes for their dolls. They could make blankets from small fabric pieces. They could also sew simple clothes and accessories.

CUP AND BALL TOY

[Makes 1]

> **Pre-Activity**: This toy was originally made from wood. The wooden ball stings when it hits a child. In this version, the ball is made from a Styrofoam ball so that it does not hurt the player. Making the cup and ball is easy. Getting the ball into the cup takes coordination and patience.

Materials

- 1 tongue depressor
- 1 paper cup
- 1 piece of string about 18 inches long
- 1 Styrofoam ball small enough to fit in cup
- sewing pin
- scissors
- hot glue gun and hot glue

Procedure

1. Make a small slit in the bottom of the paper cup with the scissors.
2. Insert the tongue depressor about 1 inch into the slit and hot glue the paper cup and tongue depressor together.
3. Tie 1 end of the string around the connection of the cup and tongue depressor.
4. Tie the other end of the string around the sewing pin. Insert the sewing pin into the Styrofoam ball and secure with a bit more hot glue.
5. Hold the toy by holding the tongue depressor handle. Swing the ball and try to catch it in the cup.

> **Post-Activity**: The Inuit have a similar toy, the iyaga, a toss and catch toy. The Inuit make their game from bones and string. Children could make an iyaga by attaching a rubber canning ring to a piece of string about 18 inches long, then tying the other end of the string to an unsharpened pencil. They hold the pencil and swing the string to catch the ring on the pencil. A more difficult variation of the game can be achieved by adding more rings to the string.

HUMMING WHIRLIGIG TOY

[Makes 1]

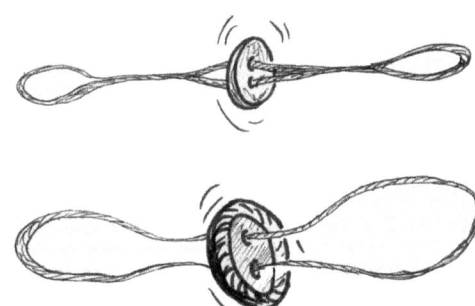

Pre-Activity: I can make these, but I cannot make them hum. Other people take my whirligigs and make them hum nicely. I cannot skip rocks either.

Materials

- ✓ flat button with at least 2 holes
- ✓ 30 inches of thread thin enough to pass through buttonholes
- ✓ scissors

Procedure

1. String the thread through the buttonholes and tie the ends. This will make a loop. The loop should be a bit longer than your body is wide.
2. Twist the thread in 1 direction until it is wound tightly.
3. Pull your arms apart and then together again. Repeat the process.
4. Soon your button will be twirling and humming.

Post-Activity: Children could investigate how different size buttons or different types of string change the humming.

QUILL PEN

[Makes 1]

Pre-Activity: Writing with a quill pen is difficult. Ink sometimes goes where it should not. It does not always go where it should. Colonial children spent about half their school day working on penmanship. Now I see why.

Materials

- ✓ goose quill or any other feather at least 11 inches long (can be obtained from craft stores or poultry farms)
- ✓ warm, soapy water in a small container
- ✓ scissors
- ✓ pin
- ✓ piece of felt about 6 inches by 6 inches
- ✓ ink
- ✓ paper

Procedure

1. Remove feathers from bottom 2 inches of quill.
2. Soak bottom of quill in warm, soapy water for about 20 minutes.
3. Cut bottom of quill off at an acute angle. This will become the nib of the pen.
4. Clean inside of nib with pin.
5. Cut a slit about a half inch long at the pointed part of the nib.
6. Dip the nib into the ink and carefully blot onto the felt to remove excess ink.
7. To write, hold the pen at a slant. This will take practice.
8. When the nib is worn down, cut quill again at an acute angle.

Post-Activity: Paper and other types of writing materials were quite rare and expensive during the colonial period. Children of that period often wrote on small chalk boards with chalk. Today's children could practice their penmanship and other types of writing on small chalk boards.

BERRY INK

[Makes about ½ cup]

Pre-Activity: Now that children have made a quill pen, they need ink. Colonial inks were often made from fireplace soot or from walnut shells. Those inks spoiled quickly, and were therefore prepared in small batches. This ink also spoils quickly, but it can be refrigerated.

Materials

- ✓ 1 cup ripe berries
- ✓ small piece of cheesecloth
- ✓ small bowl
- ✓ 1 teaspoon salt
- ✓ 1 teaspoon vinegar
- ✓ spoon
- ✓ small jar with lid

Procedure

1. Line small bowl with cheesecloth.
2. Pour berries into cheesecloth.
3. Pick up cheesecloth to make a small bag and squeeze berries so that the juices trickle into the small bowl.
4. Add vinegar and salt and stir until salt dissolves.
5. Pour the berry ink into the small jar and cap. Use as soon as possible or refrigerate for a couple of days.

Post-Activity: Children could explore other types of ink, including beet juice or concentrated grape juice.

Time Travel Culminating Activity

One child could pretend to be a person from 1776. Another child could pretend to be a current-day journalist and interview the 1776 child.

14 Let's Be Artists!

This chapter is one of my favorites! These activities harken back to ancient cultures, but they are still relevant today. Children can go on so many side trips and can circle back to these activities as they grow older.

FRESCO

[Makes 1 fresco—enough for 1 child]

Pre-Activity: A fresco is an artwork that is painted into the plaster on a wall. It becomes part of the wall and cannot be removed like a painting on canvas. First, the artist draws the work on paper. This paper is called a cartoon. Then a layer of wet plaster is applied to the wall. The cartoon is laid against the plaster and traced. Next, the artist applies the paints onto the wet plaster. When the plaster dries, the pigments become part of the plaster and thus part of the wall.

This project was originally designed using plaster of Paris. However, today experts feel plaster of Paris could cause health concerns for children. Therefore, a salt map process has been substituted for the plaster of Paris.

Materials

- 1 cup salt
- 1 cup all-purpose flour
- approximately 1 cup water
- mixing bowl
- mixing spoon
- disposable aluminum pie pan
- piece of paper size of aluminum pie pan
- pencil
- toothpicks
- egg tempera paints (see Egg Tempera Paint activity on page 97)

Procedure

1. Mix salt and flour in bowl. Add enough water, slowly and in small amounts, to make a soft dough.
2. Pour the mixture into the disposable aluminum pie pan. Smooth out the surface to make it level.
3. While the mixture hardens for a short while, draw a cartoon of final product on paper.
4. Using a toothpick, outline the design into the mixture.
5. Using another toothpick, mix some of the tempera paint into the dough. The dough and paint are now one.
6. Using new toothpicks for each new color, complete the fresco.
7. Allow fresco to harden completely.

Post-Activity: Leonardo da Vinci, Michelangelo, and Diego Rivera are among the artists who became masters of the fresco technique. Children could examine some of these artists' works. They could describe how these works are similar and how they are different.

MOSAIC

[Makes 2 mosaics]

Pre-Activity: A mosaic is an art form dating back to ancient Mesopotamia. Mosaic artifacts have been discovered in many cultures, ranging from the Persians to the Maya. In a mosaic, small pieces of stone or other materials are embedded in mortar to form an image.

This project was originally designed using plaster of Paris. However, today experts feel plaster of Paris could cause health concerns for children. Therefore, an alum dough has been substituted for the plaster of Paris. This recipe may be the perfect dough. It keeps without refrigeration for a couple of months, it dries overnight, and it does not have to be cooked.

Materials

- 3 teaspoons alum
- 1 ½ cups all-purpose flour
- 1 cup salt
- 1 cup boiling water
- 2 teaspoons vegetable oil
- mixing bowl
- mixing spoon
- mixing bowl
- mixing spoon
- 2 disposable pie pans
- cartoon (see above, Fresco project) of plan for mosaic
- items to embed in mosaic (stones, shells, beans, broken crockery, smooth pieces of glass, etc.)

Procedure

1. Combine alum, flour, and salt in mixing bowl.
2. Add boiling water and oil. Mix thoroughly.
3. Pour the mixture into 2 disposable aluminum pie pans.
4. Embed items according to cartoon.
5. Let mosaics harden for a couple of days. Remove from pans.

Post-Activity: Alum dough could be used for other projects, including imitation Mesopotamian tablets or imitations of ancient Greek busts.

Another Post-Activity: Some of today's artists combine the ideas of frescoes and mosaics. They create and paint the frescoes on walls, and then they embed mosaic pieces. Large groups of people can participate in these blendings, making their contributions very personal.

SIMPLE LOOM

[Makes 1]

> **Pre-Activity**: Just about every culture developed a simple loom. This loom is easy to make, cheap, and durable. The warp threads remain stable, and the weft threads go under and over the warp.

Materials

- ✓ 1 piece very stiff cardboard about 5 inches by 7 inches
- ✓ about 24 feet of heavy-duty string
- ✓ yarn
- ✓ ruler
- ✓ pencil
- ✓ scissors
- ✓ transparent tape

Procedure

1. With the ruler and pencil, mark off every ¼ inch along both 5-inch sides. These sides will become the ends of the looms.
2. Cut down along each mark about ½ inch to make notches.
3. Decide which side of the cardboard will be the underside of the loom. On that side tape one end of the string.
4. Wind the string around the loom and through the notches so that about 20 parallel strings now run the length of the loom. The string provides the warp for the loom.
5. Tape the end of the string on the underside of the loom.
6. Return to the top side of the loom. Cut off a piece of yarn and tie it to the extreme left string at the bottom.
7. Wind a small piece of transparent tape around the other end of the yarn, similar to the tip of a shoelace, so that the yarn will not fray.
8. Begin weaving by going over the first warp and under the next. Repeat process until you reach the end warp thread. Then reverse directions. Continue weaving until you wish to change colors or the yarn runs out.
9. When the weaving is complete, it is time to take the completed project off the loom. Return to the underside of the loom. Cut the strings along the underside.
10. Turn the loom over to the top side. Remove 2 neighboring strings from the notches and tie them together. Continue until all the strings have been removed and knotted.

⑪ The strings make a nice fringe for the weaving, or they can be trimmed.

⑫ This weaving could make a great mug mat!

Post-Activity: Children can make stripes or even more intricate patterns on their looms.

POTATO STAMPS

Pre-Activity: Children can use potato stamps to make repeating patterns. Use stamps on large pieces of paper to make wrapping paper. Many artists employ this technique on slabs of wood to create woodcuts.

Materials

- potato
- knife
- pencil
- paints and paintbrushes
- paper
- water
- paper towels

Procedure

1. Wash and dry potato.
2. Cut potato in half.
3. Draw a simple shape (such as a heart) on the cut surface of one potato half.
4. Using the knife, cut away the potato from around the design. This leaves a raised design on the cut surface.
5. Paint the raised area with paints.
6. Immediately stamp the potato on the paper.
7. Depending on the effect desired, the potato may need to be repainted every time. However, it could be used several times before needing to be repainted.

Post-Activity: As stated above, many artists employ this technique on slabs of wood to create woodcuts. Illustrator Mary Azarian earned the 1999 Caldecott Medal for her woodcut illustrations in **Snowflake Bentley**. Children could read the book, written by Jacqueline Briggs Martin, and then try to make more elaborate potato stamps.

VEGETABLE AND FRUIT STAMPS

Pre-Activity: An unusual still life can be created using these natural stamps. Mushrooms have particular appeal.

Materials

- firm vegetables or fruits, such as mushrooms, cauliflower, apples, or pears
- knife
- paints (see Chapter 15 on chromatology) and paintbrushes
- paper
- water
- paper towels

Procedure

1. Wash and dry vegetables and fruits.
2. Cut vegetables and fruits in half.
3. Paint the cut, flat areas of the fruits and vegetables with paints.
4. Immediately stamp the vegetables and fruits on the paper.
5. Depending on the effect desired, the vegetables and fruits may need to be repainted every time. However, they could be used several times before needing to be repainted.

Post-Activity: Children could view some of the portraits painted by Giuseppe Arcimboldo, born April 5, 1526. At first glance the portraits seem ordinary enough. Then second, third, and twenty-third glances show that the portraits are composed of paintings of fruits, vegetables, and other living things. His work is fascinating, especially considering the time in which he lived! Children could emulate his style by creating portraits from fruit and vegetable stamps.

Art Culminating Activity

Children could create a gallery of all their works of art.

15 Let's Be Chromatologists!

Chromatology is the study of color, so we become chromatologists when we learn about paints, pigments, and painting surfaces. The following activities are about types of paints and using paints. Paint is made by combining a pigment (color) with a binder (viscous material). The binder makes the pigment adhere to the support (paper, wood, or other materials). Several types of pigment are safe for children to use. Food coloring is transparent. However, it will not always wash out of clothes, and it can temporarily stain fingers. Watercolors are transparent and usually washable. Watercolors are easy to use by beginners, but they are actively used by professional artists. Tempera and poster paints are more opaque. They are reasonably priced and easy to obtain. They often wash out of clothing. Acrylics are more expensive, but the pigments are deep and rich. In most cases, children can interchange pigments to meet their needs.

Finger-paint paper can be bought from most craft catalogs. However, freezer paper and shelf paper are easier to obtain and work for the most part just as well. Different types of watercolor paper exist, but most of the following paints are designed to work on ordinary white drawing paper.

CLASSIC FINGER PAINT

[Makes about 2 ½ cups]

■ **Pre-Activity**: This very old recipe is worth the effort.

Materials

- ✓ 1 cup all-purpose flour
- ✓ 3 tablespoons salt
- ✓ 1 ½ cups cold water
- ✓ 1 ¼ cups hot water
- ✓ food coloring
- ✓ pot
- ✓ stove or heating element
- ✓ mixing spoon
- ✓ small containers with lids

Procedure

1. Combine flour, salt, and cold water in pot.
2. Stirring constantly, heat mixture.
3. Slowly add the hot water.
4. Stirring constantly, bring mixture to a boil. Remove from the heat when it is thick.
5. Pour some of the mixture into each of several containers. Add food coloring until desired shade is reached.
6. Store in refrigerator.

Post-Activity: Children can finger paint on either wet or dry paper. They can finger paint on finger-paint paper, or they can finger paint on regular paper.

Another Post-Activity: Children can finger paint over a resist. To make a resist, children can draw on white paper with white crayons. Then they can finger paint on the paper. The finger paint will not adhere to the areas covered with white crayons; the crayon resists the finger paint.

VERSATILE PAINT

[Makes 4 small containers of paint]

Pre-Activity: Versatile paint makes a great finger paint as well as a poster paint. It has only 2 ingredients and will keep for a long time. It provides a transparent, flat finish.

Materials

- ✓ 2 cups liquid starch
- ✓ 1 cup each of 4 colors of powdered tempera pigment
- ✓ mixing spoon
- ✓ 4 small airtight containers with lids

Procedure

1. Pour liquid starch into each of the small containers.
2. Add powdered pigments, a different color to each container.
3. Mix ingredients.

Post-Activity: This paint is also versatile because it can change uses as children age. It can start as a finger paint, then transition to a poster paint. Children could experiment with this paint and different surfaces to paint on, such as paper, canvas, wood, or ceramics. They could record how successful versatile paint was.

MILK PAINT

[Makes 1 cup]

Pre-Activity: Archaeologists have found traces of milk paint on cave walls dating back thousands of years. American colonists used milk paint to give wood a stained look and to protect the wood. Milk was cheap and easy to obtain. This version produces pastel but vibrant shades. The finish is flat and transparent. Layering it over other colors is fun. This paint does not last long even if it is refrigerated.

Materials

- ¾ cup powdered non-fat milk
- ½ cup water
- powdered tempera pigments
- mixing bowl
- mixing spoon
- several small airtight containers with lids

Procedure

1. Combine powdered milk and water in mixing bowl.
2. Pour into small containers and add powdered pigments until desired color is reached.

Post-Activity: Milk paint was used primarily on wood. Children could decorate a wooden bird house or a wooden box.

Another Post-Activity: **What if** children tried fresh whole milk instead of powdered non-fat milk in the formula?

EGG TEMPERA PAINT

[Makes 1 ¼ cups]

Pre-Activity: Egg tempera is a medium that has been used by painters from Leonardo da Vinci to Andrew Wyeth. It is opaque, but it can be thinned to any level of transparency by adding water. This paint does not last long even if it is refrigerated.

Materials

- ½ cup beaten egg yolks (4 egg yolks)
- powdered tempera pigments
- ½ cup water
- mixing spoon
- several small airtight containers with lids

Procedure

1. Pour beaten egg yolks into small containers.
2. Add powdered tempera pigments.
3. Thin with water to desired consistency.

Post-Activity: Many medieval works were painted with egg tempera. Children could find one they like and copy the style.

Another Post-Activity: Children could leave out the egg yolk and just combine pigments with water. These are the tempera paints that are often found in schools.

PAN PAINTS

[Makes ⅓ cup base to be divided into several portions, one for each color]

Pre-Activity: This mixture will foam at first. This recipe lets the children design their own watercolor colors.

Materials

- 3 tablespoons cornstarch
- 3 tablespoons baking soda
- 3 tablespoons white vinegar
- 2 teaspoons light corn syrup
- food coloring
- mixing bowl
- mixing spoon
- several containers with lids

Procedure

1. Combine cornstarch, baking soda, white vinegar, and light corn syrup in mixing bowl.
2. Place a small amount of the mixture into each of several containers.
3. Add food coloring to achieve desired shade.
4. Use as is or wait until they dry into pan paints.

Post-Activity: Children could compare and contrast their homemade paints with commercially produced paints that they might own.

Another Post-Activity: Watercolor pencils provide a wonderful variety of painting opportunities. Children can wet the paper before using them. They can wet the pencil. They can draw dry on dry paper and then add water. Children can make a very useful watercolor book with watercolor pencils. First, they need a small book made from plain paper or watercolor paper. Then they choose one color watercolor pencil and create a block of that color on one of the book pages. They should press very hard to apply lots of pigment to the paper. Then they can add other colors to that page or to other pages. To use, children dip a paintbrush in water and then pick up some of the pigment from the book. They then paint on different paper.

Chromatology Culminating Activity

Children could create a large color wheel of the colors they have created. They could turn that color wheel into an object, for example a large flower where every petal is a different color on the color wheel. They could also learn about primary and secondary colors and how and when to use them.

16 Let's Be Clayologists!

Clays and doughs can be divided into two groups: those that dry and those that do not dry. A clay or dough that dries will retain its shape and can be used to make permanent projects. A dough that does not dry may keep its shape if left undisturbed. However, it can be used only for temporary activities. Most of the recipes included here will dry. Each recipe will indicate whether the clay will dry or not.

The following clays and doughs do not require a kiln. Clays and doughs can clog a sink, so all such materials should be thrown away in the trash.

SILLY STUFF

[Makes 2 ¼ cups—enough for 2 children]

Pre-Activity: Silly stuff is similar to Play Doh®. Silly stuff is for temporary use; it does not dry well.

Materials

- 1 cup all-purpose flour
- ½ cup salt
- 2 tablespoons vegetable oil
- 1 cup water
- 2 teaspoons cream of tartar
- food coloring (optional)
- stove or heating element
- pot
- mixing spoon
- airtight storage container

Procedure

1. Mix all ingredients in pot.
2. Cook over medium heat, stirring until mixture sticks together in a ball.
3. Remove pot from heat and let dough cool.
4. Squeeze and knead. Have fun!
5. Store in airtight container.

Post-Activity: Children could create their own extruders and experiment. For example, silly stuff could be pushed through an old sieve to create silly stuff spaghetti.

Another Post-Activity: They could create silly stuff pretend foods. For example, they could form some tan silly stuff into the shape of a slice of bread. Then they could top the pretend bread with some pretend strawberry jam.

PLAYFUL PLASTIC

[Makes about a cup—enough to make several small objects]

Pre-Activity: Similar to Plasticine®, playful plastic is for temporary use. It does not dry well. This clay can be used for stop-motion photography.

Materials

- 4 ounces beeswax, grated
- 5 old crayons
- 2 tablespoons petroleum jelly
- old double boiler that will never cook food again
- old mixing spoon
- stove or heating element
- water
- wax paper

Procedure

1. Pour grated beeswax into smaller pot of double boiler.
2. Pour water into larger portion of double boiler.
3. Place smaller portion of double boiler into larger portion.
4. Place double boiler onto stove and melt wax.
5. Remove paper from crayons and add crayons to melting wax.
6. When wax and crayons have melted, remove double boiler from stove. Add petroleum jelly and let the mixture cool for 30 minutes.
7. Remove mixture from double boiler and place on wax paper. Have fun!

Post-Activity: The author Barbara Reid uses Plasticine® to create scenes that are then photographed to become the illustrations in her books. Children could read several of her books. I particularly like *Sing a Song of Bedtime*. They could try to emulate her style.

FLOUR CLAY

[Makes 6 cups—enough for 3 children]

> **Pre-Activity**: Flour clay requires no cooking. It is versatile in that it can be baked or allowed to air dry. Children can make thin coils of clay and intertwine them to make baskets. Children can also make "bagels" and other bread look-alikes. Flour clay projects can last for years and can be painted after the clay has dried.

Materials

- ✓ 4 cups all-purpose flour
- ✓ 1 ½ cups warm water
- ✓ 1 cup salt
- ✓ mixing bowl
- ✓ mixing spoon
- ✓ baking sheet
- ✓ refrigerator

Procedure

1. Thoroughly mix flour, water, and salt in mixing bowl and refrigerate for 30 minutes.
2. Make relatively thin baskets, decorations, or other projects.
3. Place on baking sheet. Air dry for several days or bake at 300°F for 1 hour.
4. Refrigerate any unused clay in a plastic bag.

> **Post-Activity**: Children could open a pretend store and sell their items.

FROZEN BREAD MOLDING MATERIAL

[Makes enough for 4 children]

Pre-Activity: This dough can be expensive. Watch for sales of frozen bread dough. Baking produces hard-finished items that cannot be eaten.

Materials

- ✓ 1 loaf frozen bread dough
- ✓ 1 egg white
- ✓ 2 teaspoons water
- ✓ baking sheet
- ✓ nonstick cooking spray
- ✓ small mixing bowl
- ✓ fork
- ✓ brush

Procedure

1. Defrost bread dough the day before using.
2. Break dough into smaller portions and shape as desired.
3. Place creations on baking sheet sprayed with nonstick cooking spray.
4. Let rise for about 1 hour.
5. Beat egg white and water together in the small mixing bowl with the fork.
6. Brush egg white on creations.
7. Bake at 350°F for about 15–20 minutes.

Post-Activity: This dough is great for science fair activities, for example a diorama of the planets. Another project would be what various molecules, for example water, look like.

CINNAMON DOUGH

[Makes about 1 ½ cups]

Pre-Activity: The smell is wonderful! It does not easily dry out. Consider making Christmas items from the material. The final products are not edible.

Materials

- 1 cup all-purpose flour
- ½ cup salt
- 2 teaspoons cream of tartar
- 2 teaspoons vegetable oil
- 1 cup water
- about 6 drops red food coloring
- about 6 drops green food coloring
- 2 tablespoons ground cinnamon
- 2 tablespoons ground allspice
- 2 mixing bowls
- 2 mixing spoons
- old pot
- stove or heating element
- kneading surface with extra flour
- airtight container

Procedure

1. Mix flour, salt, and cream of tartar in a bowl.
2. Stir in cinnamon and allspice.
3. In the other bowl, add the food colorings to the water. Red and green should form brown.
4. Add water mixture and vegetable oil to dry ingredients and stir.
5. Pour into old pot and cook mixture for about 3 minutes, stirring constantly.
6. Remove dough from pot and knead until it is pliable and smooth.
7. Allow to cool.
8. Shape as desired and let air dry.
9. Store any unused dough in airtight container.

Post-Activity: Children could substitute unsweetened applesauce for most of the water in the recipe. This should make a tighter dough. They could then take cookie cutters and fill them with a flat layer of dough. They could also make a hole at the top of the dough with a straw. When the dough dries, children can remove the cookie shape from the cookie cutter, insert a ribbon through the hole, and hang these sweet-smelling decorations on Christmas trees.

Clayology Culminating Activity

Children could display the objects they have made, including things from other chapters, for example the volcano model. They could rank their favorite clay and their least favorite clay. They could also experiment with natural clay.

17 Let's Be Paper Chemists!

Paper originated about 2,000 years ago. The Chinese were the first to discover how to make paper. Before that, papyrus, vellum, parchment, bark, clay, and various other materials were used as writing surfaces. Paper is the result of beating plant fibers, bringing forth the cellulose in those fibers, adding water, and sieving the mixture, which is called slurry.

Making new paper from old paper and other materials is fun, but it is also messy and it takes practice. First products are generally quite thick and resemble the material from which egg cartons are made.

Mold and Deckle

The mold, basically a sieve, strains paper fibers from slurry. The deckle, which snaps onto the mold, frames the new paper and keeps the paper fibers on the mold as it is lifted from the slurry. Mold and deckle sets are available at craft stores and through art supply catalogs. If you do not wish to purchase a mold and deckle set, you can easily make your own.

TRADITIONAL RECTANGULAR MOLD AND DECKLE

[Makes 1]

Pre-Activity: This process takes quite a bit of time, but the mold and deckle are quite sturdy.

Materials

- window screening, 12 inches by 14 inches
- wood molding
- nails
- staple gun and staples

Procedure

1. Make two frames from wood molding and nails. Make one frame 10 inches by 12 inches. Make the other frame slightly smaller.
2. Wrap window screening around larger of 2 frames.
3. Staple window screening onto frame to make the mold.
4. The other frame (without screening) is the deckle.

Post-Activity: A simple mold and deckle can be made from two picture frames and a piece of plastic canvas. One picture frame must be larger than the other. Hot glue the plastic canvas to the larger picture frame to become the mold. The smaller picture frame will become the deckle.

Paper and Paper Products

BASIC RECYCLED PAPER

Pre-Activity: Plan 2 days for this project. Children love the mess, and they are amazed they can actually make paper.

Materials

- newspaper
- warm water
- bucket
- scoop
- blender
- mold and deckle
- old dishpan wider than mold and deckle
- damp cloth

Procedure

1. Tear newspaper into pieces the size of quarters. Place pieces into bucket.
2. Add warm water to cover the paper. Soak paper overnight in bucket.
3. The next day, scoop 1 cup of paper into blender. Cover with water. Blend until pulpy. This combination of pulp and water is called slurry.
4. Add more paper and blend again.
5. Pour slurry into dishpan.
6. Repeat process until dishpan is half full.
7. Slide mold and deckle through slurry until screen rests on bottom of dishpan.
8. With both hands, raise mold and deckle. A great deal of slurry should stay on the mold as it is raised.
9. Press slurry to get rid of water and to distribute slurry evenly.
10. When desired shape and thickness are attained, remove deckle. Flip mold over damp cloth. The new paper will fall onto damp cloth.
11. Repeat process to make more sheets of paper.
12. Allow paper to dry. Remove from cloth.

Post-Activity: Children can make rag paper by adding 1 cup of dryer lint to every half-gallon of slurry.

Another Post-Activity: Children can make nature paper by adding elements of nature, such as pine needles, flower petals, and herbs to the slurry.

DECORATIVE PAPER CONTAINERS

Pre-Activity: Recycled paper is similar to papier mâché in that it can be shaped over containers. When dry, it takes the shape of the container. The finished product is not waterproof.

Materials

- ✓ materials from "Basic Recycled Paper" (see process on previous page)
- ✓ scoop
- ✓ sieve
- ✓ small bowl, plate, or container to serve as mold
- ✓ scissors
- ✓ paints (see Chapter 15 on chromatology) and paintbrushes (optional)

Procedure

1. Follow directions for "Basic Recycled Paper." However, do not use mold and deckle.
2. Remove a scoopful of slurry and drain water by using sieve.
3. Apply slurry to small bowl, plate, or another container and press it around the container either on the inside or the outside.
4. If the slurry is molded around the inside of the container, the finished product will be rough on the inside and smooth on the outside.
5. If the slurry is molded around the outside of the container, the finished product will be rough on the outside and smooth on the inside.
6. Let stand for 1 day. Remove original container and trim edges of finished product with scissors.
7. Paint if desired. See Chapter 15 on chromatology for some ideas regarding paint.

Post-Activity: Children could upcycle empty food jars into vases or pencil cups by applying the slurry to the outsides of the jars. They could paint the new object when the slurry has dried.

DECKLED PAPER

Pre-Activity: One way to age paper is to deckle the edges. The paper's edges will look frayed, typical of old paper.

Materials

- ✓ 1 sheet of paper with a message written on it
- ✓ water
- ✓ sponge
- ✓ ruler

Procedure

1. Slightly dampen edges of the paper with a sponge.
2. Place a ruler on the paper, parallel to and near the paper's edge.
3. Hold the ruler down firmly with one hand and tear the paper against the ruler with the other hand. The paper will have a ragged edge.
4. Let the paper dry.

Post-Activity: This activity would be a great add-on to one of the invisible inks. Children could deckle the paper and then add an invisible ink to create a pirate treasure map.

AGED PAPER

Pre-Activity: This process makes new paper look old. Children can use the technique to age newly created letters, maps, or diary entries.

Materials

- ✓ 2 cups fairly hot coffee or tea
- ✓ written project such as a letter, map, or diary entry
- ✓ large bowl
- ✓ newspaper

Procedure

1. Pour coffee or tea into a bowl.
2. Crumple the written project and submerge in coffee or tea.
3. Let soak for a short time. The longer the soak, the darker the tint. However, the paper also becomes more fragile.
4. Remove paper from liquid and dry on newspaper.

Post-Activity: This activity would be a great add-on to one of the invisible inks. Children could age the paper and then add an invisible ink to create a long-lost code.

Paper Chemistry Culminating Activity

Artists often make portfolios of their works. Here children could make a portfolio of all the different types of paper they made.

18 Let's Be Paper Engineers!

Sheets of paper can be folded into all kinds of interesting experiments and artistic expressions. Again, many of these activities have been around for decades, but they lend themselves to further experimentation involving critical thinking and creativity.

PINWHEEL

[Makes 1]

Pre-Activity: This project has been around for a very long time. A windy spring morning would be great weather for pinwheels.

Materials

- 1 piece square card stock about 10 inches on each side
- scissors
- 1 straight pin
- 1 pencil with a soft eraser

Procedure

1. Fold card stock on 1 diagonal to make a triangle. Press to make a crease.
2. Open card stock and fold on other diagonal. Press to make a crease.
3. Open card stock again.
4. The center is where the 2 folds meet.
5. Cut along the folds close to but not through the center. You should have 4 triangles joined at the center.
6. Take 1 of corner cuts and bring it to the center. Hold it in place.
7. Do the same for the corresponding corners of the other 3 triangles.
8. Push straight pin through corners, through the center, and into the pencil eraser.
9. Make sure the straight pin allows the pinwheel to turn freely.

Post-Activity: Children can decorate the card stock before it is bent, cut, and fastened. Specifically, they could use red, white, and blue colors to make a July 4th project. They could make spring-themed or fall-themed pinwheels.

VERTICAL SPINNERS

[Makes 1]

Pre-Activity: This project, amazingly simple to set up, produces such excitement. This experiment lends itself to many further investigations. Children can devote quite a few science sessions to setting up and conducting experiments.

Materials

- ✓ 1 piece of card stock about 2 inches by 6 inches
- ✓ medium-size paper clip
- ✓ scissors

Procedure

1. Hold the card stock on 1 long side and cut down 1 short end about 2 ⅕ inches.
2. About an inch below that cut, snip the two long sides about ¾ inch each.
3. Go back to the first cut and fold 1 flap in 1 direction and the other flap the other direction. These form the "wings" of the twirler.
4. Now go to the second cut. From 1 cut fold the paper lengthwise in the direction opposite that of its corresponding wing.
5. Fold the paper lengthwise from the other small cut in the direction opposite that of its corresponding wing.
6. Fold up bottom inch of twirler and add a paper clip.
7. Hold twirler as high as possible just under wings and drop it. It spins as it drops.

Post-Activity: Children could add more paper clips. They could shorten the wings. They could make it from other materials.

Another Post-Activity: They could drop 2 spinners, one significantly larger than the other, at the same time. Do they hit the floor at the same time? Do Newton's Laws of Gravity apply here?

HORIZONTAL SPINNERS

[Makes 1]

Pre-Activity: This project also causes great excitement. Can we make it smaller? How big can we make it? Does it work without paper clips?

Materials

✓ 1 strip of card stock, 1 inch by 7 inches   ✓ 1 paper clip

Procedure

1. Fold card stock in half so that it is 1 inch by 3 ½ inches.
2. Approximately 1 inch from the fold end fold down the end at a 45° angle.
3. Approximately 1 inch from the unfolded end fold down the end at a 45° angle but in the opposite direction from the other end.
4. Fasten paper clip in middle of paper.
5. Open the 2 ends slightly to form wings.
6. Drop paper and watch it spin.

Post-Activity: Children could change the size of the spinner. They could make it from various types of paper.

PAPER WREATH OR STAR OR FLOWER

[Makes 1]

Pre-Activity: The trick is in the last fold and the glue. A Christmas wreath could be made from green construction paper, and red mistletoe berries (either real or paper) could be added. A star can be made by pinching the ends. Glitter can easily be glued on.

Materials

- ✓ 1 piece of construction paper, 12 inches by 18 inches
- ✓ scissors
- ✓ glue
- ✓ stapler and staples

Procedure

1. Fold the paper in half horizontally so that the long ends meet.
2. Fold 1 long edge down about an inch.
3. Fold the other long edge down about an inch but in the other direction.
4. Make quite a few cuts from the middle fold to these new folds. Each new cut should be about ¾ of an inch away from the previous cut.
5. Unfold paper and reverse paper so that the previous inside is now the outside.
6. Lay 1 short edge over the other so that a tube is formed. Glue the overlapped edges together.
7. Bring ends of tube together to form wreath and staple 2 ends together.
8. Decorate and enjoy.

Post-Activity: Children could make some small spring flowers and add paper leaves and pipe cleaner stems.

ORIGAMI FORTUNE TELLER

[Makes 1]

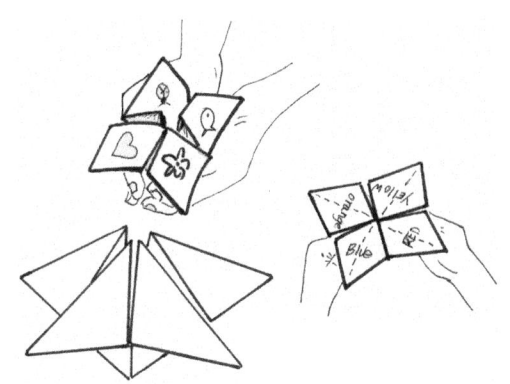

> **Pre-Activity**: The fortune teller, also called various other names, has been around for hundreds of years. It is a form of origami. Children could change the message to create more fun.

Materials

- ✓ 1 piece of square paper at least 8 ½ inches by 8 ½ inches
- ✓ markers

Procedure

1. Fold the paper in diagonal and make a crease.
2. Open paper and fold opposite diagonal and crease.
3. Unfold paper. Fold each of 4 corners to center of paper (where diagonals cross).
4. Turn paper over and fold those 4 corners to center.
5. Number each of the small triangles.
6. Under each triangle write a different message.
7. Turn fortune teller over and write the name of a color in each corner.
8. Fold fortune teller in half so that the colors are on the outside.
9. Fold fortune teller in half the opposite way. Repeat steps 8 and 9 until fortune teller folds easily.
10. Place thumb and index finger of each hand into the pockets created where the colors are written. You are ready to tell fortunes!

> **Post-Activity**: Children could add illustrations, use different color papers, add different messages. They could also add stickers (see Make Your Own Stickers, page 123).

Paper Engineering Culminating Activity

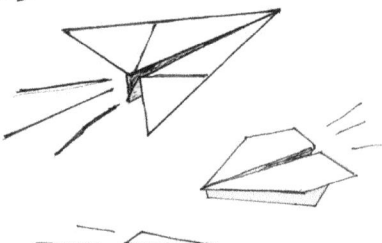

Children could create contests regarding the paper activities in this chapter. Which vertical spinner spun the fastest? Which Christmas wreath was the most elaborate? Children could include other paper activities not mentioned in this book, for example paper airplanes.

19 Let's Be Crafters!

Sometimes children need a project to do right now and right here! Sometimes they have school projects that must be done tonight! These 5 activities are easy to set up, easy to complete, and easy to have fun with.

SCRATCH-AND-SNIFF PAINTS

[Makes 2 tablespoons]

Pre-Activity: Children like scratch-and-sniff activities. This recipe is easy to make.

Materials

- 2 tablespoons unsweetened powdered drink mix
- 1 tablespoon warm water
- small paper cups
- mixing spoon
- paintbrush and paper

Procedure

1. Combine drink mix and water in cup.
2. Paint on paper.
3. Allow surface to dry for 24 hours before scratching and sniffing.

Post-Activity: Children could make their own Valentines and add a scratch and sniff accent. They could also make birthday cards or Christmas cards with a lovely smell.

SCRATCH-OFF PROJECTS

[Makes potentially many, many]

Pre-Activity: This project is similar to lottery ticket scratch-offs.

Materials

- card stock
- medium-tipped marker
- small piece of clear packing tape
- silver or dark color acrylic paint
- paintbrush
- coin

Procedure

1. Write a message on the card stock with marker. Surround message with a border.
2. Apply packing tape over the message and border.
3. Paint over the packing tape with silver or dark color acrylic paint. Let dry. Another layer or so of paint may be necessary to cover the message.
4. To reveal the message, scrape the paint with the coin. Voila! The message has returned.

Post-Activity: Ideas for its use are endless: homemade Valentine messages, Mother's Day coupon books, and chore books are just a few ideas.

COLORED GLUES AND/OR GLITTER GLUES

Pre-Activity: Glue makers are now selling colored glues. These colored glues add spice to posters and other projects. Glitter glues produce puffy, interesting touches to projects. Homemade glitter glues and colored glues are easy to make and are usually cheaper than purchased glues. Glitter, as always, can end up in unexpected places.

Materials

✓ white glue in squeeze bottles

✓ poster paint

Procedure

1. Open bottles of glue.
2. For colored glues, add a bit of poster paint to each bottle. Replace lids and shake. The finished product will be darker colored than the original paint. Do not add too much paint, or the liquid will affect the glue's effectiveness.
3. For a variation, do not shake the bottle too much. The marbled glue will produce interesting results.
4. For glitter glues, add a bit of glitter to each bottle. Replace lids and shake.

Post-Activity: Children could create a selection of colored/glitter glues on hand. They can also really customize colors. Who knows when you will need teal-colored glue with silver glitter?

MAKE YOUR OWN STICKERS

[Makes many]

■ **Pre-Activity**: This activity really encourages creativity.

Materials

- ✓ drawing paper
- ✓ markers or colored pencils
- ✓ scissors
- ✓ 1 piece parchment paper
- ✓ clear packing tape

Procedure

1. Create images for stickers on drawing paper. Use markers or colored pencils to add further creativity. Cut out what will become stickers.
2. Place about a 6-inch length of packing tape sticky side down on parchment paper.
3. Place stickers face up on top of the packing tape.
4. Place another 6-inch length of packing tape on top of the soon-to-be stickers, sandwiching the decorated paper between 2 layers of tape.
5. Peel bottom layer of packing tape from parchment paper.
6. Cut out stickers. Any stickers not to be placed on other surfaces can be stored on parchment paper.

■ **Post-Activity**: Did you know you can buy sticker paper? Who knew? Sticker paper may be easier to use, but the method used here needs no run to the craft store.

SNOW GLOBE

[Makes 1]

Pre-Activity: The glycerin changes the water slightly so that the glitter drifts down slowly. Glycerin can be purchased at a pharmacy.

Materials

- 1 small, clear jar with tight-fitting lid
- 1 small toy or figure
- tacky glue (waterproof)
- distilled water
- several drops of glycerin
- glitter or plastic confetti

Procedure

1. Glue figure or toy to inside of lid with tacky glue. Let it dry overnight.
2. Fill jar almost to the top with distilled water. Add several drops of glycerin.
3. Add glitter or plastic confetti.
4. Spread glue around the top of jar.
5. Screw lid on and let glue dry.

Post-Activity: Light corn syrup or baby oil could be substituted for glycerin. Children could figure out why distilled water is necessary for this activity.

Another Post-Activity: We associate snow globes with winter holidays. However, children could create a Halloween or a Thanksgiving or an Easter globe.

Crafting Culminating Activity

Children could pretend they own a craft store and produce a commercial to convince people to buy their products.

20 Let's Be Wackadoodle Scientists!

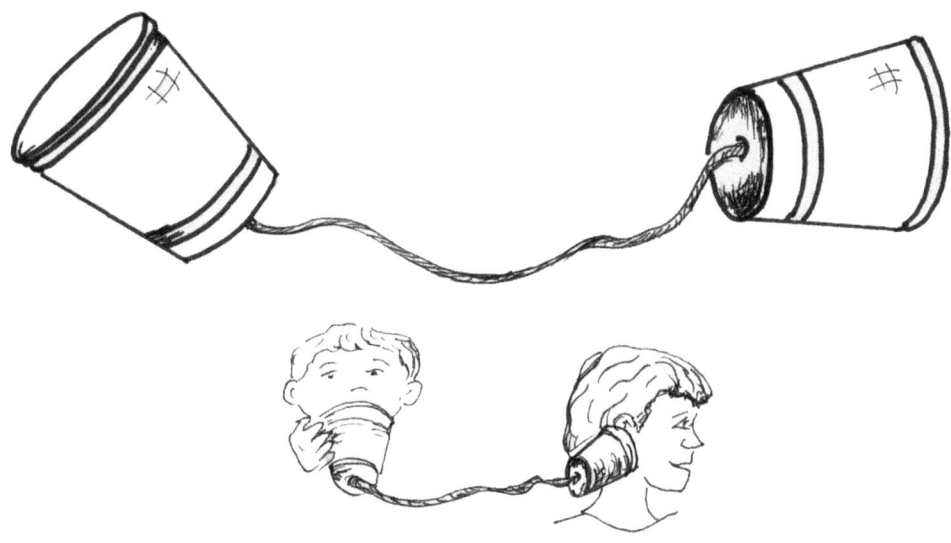

My book *The BIG Book of Glues, Brews, and Goos: 500+ Kid-Tested Recipes and Formulas for Hands-On Learning* is like an encyclopedia, featuring lots of different activities. My publisher asked me to choose 100 of those activities for this book. That was very difficult, because I had obviously more than 500 wonderful activities to choose from. In addition, those activities had to relate to interesting topics. That was difficult as well. I had 5 great activities that could not fit into any of those topics, so I decided to group them together under Wackadoodle Science. Enjoy these activities just to enjoy!

CANDY-DIET SODA ERUPTION

[Makes 1]

> **Pre-Activity**: This eruption must be done outside on a warm day! The eruption can be up to about 8 feet high. The person completing the last step must be a fast runner!

Materials

- ✓ 1 roll Mentos® candies
- ✓ 1 2-liter bottle diet soda at room temperature
- ✓ 1 sheet writing paper

Procedure

1. Roll the sheet of paper into a tube that is as big as the diameter of the candies.
2. Unwrap the candies.
3. Find an open spot outside. Place bottle of diet soda on the ground and remove the cap.
4. Place 5 candies into the tube. Place your hand over bottom of tube so that the candies do not roll out.
5. Place tube in bottle opening. Let the candies roll into the bottle.
6. Run like crazy and watch the eruption!

> **Post-Activity**: This eruption happens on a grand scale. Children could make mini-eruptions (still outside) by placing 1 candy in a smaller bottle of soda. They could experiment with different types of soda and different candies.

DANCING RAISINS

[Makes 1 demonstration]

> **Pre-Activity**: The raisins rise when the soda's carbon dioxide bubbles are caught in the raisin's wrinkly skin. When the raisins reach the soda's surface, the carbon dioxide bubbles break. The raisins sink until they catch another carbon dioxide bubble. When carbon dioxide bubbles no longer rise, the raisins no longer dance.

Materials

- ✓ clear soda or seltzer
- ✓ about 10 raisins
- ✓ tall, clear glass

Procedure

1. Pour soda or seltzer into glass.
2. Drop the raisins in the liquid.
3. Watch the raisins start to fall. Then watch the raisins rise and fall, rise and fall.

> **Post-Activity**: Children could conduct different experiments. Do older raisins with more wrinkles dance more than newer, plumper raisins? Does diet soda, containing more carbonation than regular soda, encourage more dancing? Does other fruit dance?

BALLOON ROCKET

[Makes 1]

Pre-Activity: The project is best completed with a friend. It also lends itself to so many experimental side trips.

Materials

- ✓ 1 length of string at least 10 feet long, enough to be tied to strong furniture pieces or attached to opposite walls
- ✓ 1 straw
- ✓ 2 large paperclips
- ✓ 1 balloon
- ✓ masking tape

Procedure

1. Thread the string through the straw and attach string to furniture or walls. Make sure the string is taut and level.
2. Unbend each paperclip so that each roughly has the letter S shape.
3. Hook the paper clips over the straw and tape in place.
4. Carefully tape the other ends of the paperclips to the balloon so that balloon opening is near 1 piece of furniture or 1 wall.
5. Inflate the balloon and pinch closed the end of the balloon.
6. Release the balloon. As the balloon's air exits through the opening, the balloon and straw will travel the opposite direction along the string. Did the balloon reach the other piece of furniture or wall?

Post-Activity: How could the experiment be improved? Different string or even fishing line? Long balloon as opposed to round ballon? Shorter straw? All good thinking!

STRAW ROCKET

[Makes 1]

Pre-Activity: The paper rocket dimensions and fins are intentionally vague, allowing young scientists to exercise creativity and critical thinking.

Materials

- ✓ 1 straw
- ✓ 1 pencil
- ✓ 1 piece printer paper
- ✓ scotch tape
- ✓ scissors

Procedure

1. Cut a rectangle from the printer paper that is big enough to wrap around the top half of the pencil, including the point. Tape the ends together.
2. Squish the portion around the point to make the rocket nose cone.
3. Cut out some fins and tape them on the bottom of the paper rocket.
4. Remove pencil and insert straw.
5. Blow into the end of the straw. How far does the rocket travel?

Post-Activity: How could children modify their rockets to increase travel distance? Does aiming the rocket at different vertical angles change the distance?

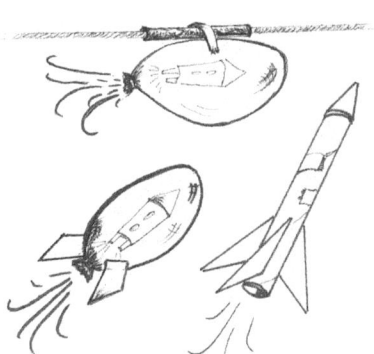

SIMPLE TELEPHONES

[Makes 1 set]

Pre-Activity: Today's children, growing up with cell phones, may not understand how original telephones worked. They are intrigued with the idea of sound traveling along a string.

Materials

- ✓ 2 paper or plastic cups
- ✓ 10 feet of heavy-duty string
- ✓ scissors

Procedure

1. With scissors, punch a small hole in bottom of each cup.
2. Push one end of string through hole from the bottom into the cup.
3. Tie a knot in the string so that the string cannot slip out of the bottom of the cup.
4. Do the same for the other cup.
5. Now the string connects both cups, the telephones.
6. Pull string taut.
7. One child should talk into the cup, and the other child should listen. Then they can change roles.

Post-Activity: Children could see if these phones work when the string goes around corners. Could they add more lines to the phones? What if the string is not taut? How long can the string be to still work?

Wackadoodle Science Culminating Activity

Children could pretend to be a famous scientist who has a series of videos. They could create videos of themselves performing their experiments.

Bibliography

Andrews, Gavin. *500 Kids Art Ideas: Inspiring Projects for Fostering Creativity and Self-Expression.* Beverly, MA: Quarry Books, 2015.

Audubon, John James and Sibley, David. *The Birds of America.* Munich, Germany: Prestel, 2021.

Carle, Eric. *The Very Hungry Caterpillar.* New York: Penguin Random House, 1994.

Chatterton, Crystal. *Awesome Science Experiments for Kids: 100+ Fun STEM /STEAM Projects and Why They Work.* Emeryville, CA: Rockridge Press, 2018.

Corfee, Stephanie. *Craft Lab for Kids: 52 DIY Projects to Inspire, Excite, and Empower Kids to Create Useful, Beautiful Handmade Goods.* Beverly, MA: Quarry Books, 2020.

Daniels, Jaret C. *Insects and Bugs Backyard Workbook: Hands-On Projects, Quizzes, and Activities for Kids.* Cambridge, MN: Adventures Publications, 2021.

Elzer-Peters, Katie. *Kitchen Gardening for Beginners: Regrow Your Leftover Greens, Stalks, Seeds, and More.* Dover, DE: New Shoe Press, 2024.

Marks, Diana F. *The BIG Book of Glues, Brews, and Goos: 500+ Kid-Tested Recipes and Formulas for Hands-On Learning.* Santa Barbara, CA: Libraries Unlimited, 2015.

Martin, Jacqueline Briggs. *Snowflake Bentley.* New York: Houghton Mifflin, 1998.

Reader's Digest. *For the Birds: Easy-to-Make Recipes for your Feathered Friends.* Pleasantville, NY: The Reader's Digest Association, Inc., 2010.

Reid, Barbara. *Sing a Song of Bedtime.* Toronto, Canada: North Winds Press, 2015.

Robbins, Crystal. *Kitchen Chemists: Fun Experiments for Curious Kids.* Independently published, 2023.

Satler, Helen Roney. *Recipes for Art and Craft Materials.* New York: Lothrop, Lee & Shepard; William Morrow, 1973.

Seuss, Dr. *Bartholomew and the Oobleck.* New York: Random House Books for Young Readers, 1949.

Sheinmel, Courtney. *My Pet Slime.* Kansas City, MO: Andrews McMeel Publishing, 2020.

Spangler, Steve. *Smithsonian 10-Minute Science Experiments: 50+ Quick, Easy and Awesome Projects for Kids.* New York: Media Lab Books, 2019.

Yi, Andrea Scalzo. *100 Easy STEAM Activities: Awesome Hands-On Projects for Aspiring Artists and Engineers.* Salem, MA: Page Street Books, 2019.

www.ingramcontent.com/pod-product-compliance
Ingram Content Group UK Ltd.
Pitfield, Milton Keynes, MK11 3LW, UK
UKHW051918290126
467490UK00010B/327